P.G. WODEHOUSE

P.G. WODEHOUSE

AN ILLUSTRATED BIOGRAPHY

With Complete Bibliography and Collector's Guide

JOSEPH CONNOLLY

EEL
PIE
PUBLISHING

First published by Orbis Publishing Limited 1979

This edition first published 1981 by
Eel Pie Publishing Limited, 45 Broadwick Street, London W1V 1FS.

ISBN 0 906008 44 1

Printed and bound in Great Britain by
R. J. Acford, Industrial Estate, Chichester, Sussex.

FRONTISPIECE: *Plum at home. In his eighties, and enjoying America.*
In the background, part of the Autograph *edition of his work is visible.*

CONTENTS

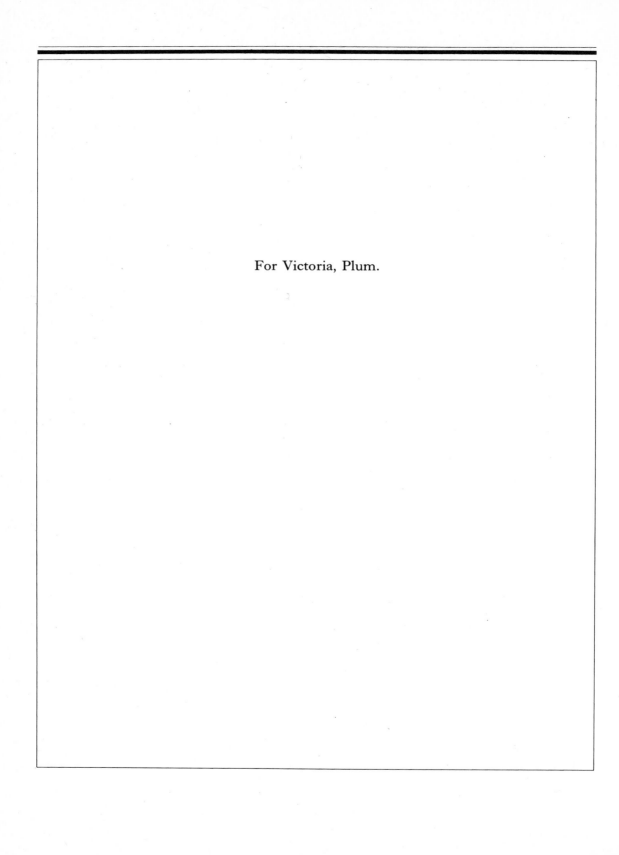

For Victoria, Plum.

FOREWORD

It is tempting, I suppose, to wonder whether some melancholic skulked behind the clown's mask, or even whether Wodehouse's comic writing veiled some deeper motivation or private tragedy. No. Wodehouse was not deep. Although he greatly loved and admired Shakespeare, and read him every day, he had no desire to write another Hamlet. As has been stated elsewhere so lucidly and unequivocally, he had no message.

All Wodehouse did, if his achievement may be thought of as in any sense mere, was write a far greater number of consistently funny books than anyone else in the history of literature. And he did it superbly well. And he enjoyed it most utterly.

The truth is that behind the happy face there lurked a happy man.

Joseph Connolly Hampstead. 1979.

P. G. Wodehouse

ACKNOWLEDGMENTS

I am greatly indebted to the Estate of the late P. G. Wodehouse, and to Messrs A. P. Watt, for permission to quote from Wodehouse's works, notably *Performing Flea* (Herbert Jenkins).

I should also like to thank the Dulwich College Library for their courtesy, and for making available all sorts of things.

My thanks are also due to Collins Publishers for permission to quote from Malcolm Muggeridge's *The Infernal Grove*, to Mrs Sonia Brownwell Orwell for permission to quote from George Orwell's *Critical Essays* (Martin Secker & Warburg Ltd), to Mr Philip Norman for permission to quote from *Thank You, Plum (Sunday Times)*, and to Mr Auberon Waugh for permission to quote from his writings in the *New Statesman*.

I also acknowledge the assistance of *The Alleynian, The Times*, the British Broadcasting Corporation, the National Book League, the London Library, the American Library, Oxford University, Mr David Jasen, Mr Richard Usborne, and Mr Peter Schwed of Simon and Schuster.

CHAPTER ONE

THE LITTLE NUGGET

"Do you really want to hear the story of my life, Biscuit?" he said wistfully. "Sure it won't bore you?"
"Bore me? My dear chap! I'm agog. Let's have the whole thing. Start from the beginning. Childhood –
early surroundings – genius probably inherited from male grand-parent – push along."
BIG MONEY

As far as the eye could reach, I found myself gazing on a surging sea of aunts.
THE MATING SEASON

"If I had my life to live again, Jeeves, I would start it as an orphan without any aunts. Don't they put
aunts in Turkey in sacks and drop them in the Bosphorus?"
"Odalisques, sir, I understand. Not aunts."
THE CODE OF THE WOOSTERS

He would have won no prizes for physical beauty. The head was a large affair, with the rather unexceptional features tending to clutter up the centre. His hair, always very short, had by his mid-twenties reverted to a semi-transparent sort of baby-fluff, beneath which the jaw loomed reasonably massive. And neither did the pink and totally functional spectacles help. But kindness is the keynote here – kindness and good humour shine through even the worst of his photographs. He smiled a lot – usually, in fact. He was over six feet tall, and had two large hands and two large feet on the ends of the limbs you would expect. Sartorially speaking, he was nowhere, in his later years assuming the uniform of American suburban man, short-sleeved, usually checked, shirt, and comfy bags fastened across the stomach. Wodehouse, naturally, was fully aware of all this, and was quite genuinely mystified and more than slightly appalled when anyone requested his photograph, or if he was invited to appear on television – which he was, often, and which he did almost never. He was not over-struck by his own voice either, feeling quite at a loss as to why anyone should be inclined to part with the hard-earned in exchange for a gramophone record of Wodehouse Reading – or, as he put it, droning on and on.

With some of which, people may agree. But Wodehouse's fans do not give a jot for

Dust-wrapper design by Rex Whistler from the first edition of Louder and Funnier *(1932)*

any of the above, and rightly. Is not the man himself the thing? The man, and his books? Yes he is, yes they are.

P.G. Wodehouse was born in 1881, which surprised no-one very much as he had been expected for some time. What was rather a surprise, though, was the fact that he greeted the world from Guildford, Surrey, when the family had been living in Hong Kong for many years. P.G.'s father, Henry Ernest Wodehouse, was in the Civil Service, and in this capacity had gone to Hong Kong in 1867, where ten years later he married one Eleanor Deane, a Reverend's daughter from Bath. That same year, they had a son, Philip Peveril. Two years later, they had another, Ernest Armine. A couple of years after that, the time might have seemed right to make up the hat-trick, and another son was born. Eleanor was visiting a friend in Guildford at the time, and by most accounts it would appear that this third son was a little over-eager to partake of whatever was going on, and was born on the 15th of October, before you could boil a kettle. Pelham Grenville was the name. After the godfather Colonel Pelham Grenville von Donop, so you see it could just have been worse. A couple of Wodehouse's school friends later recalled that they called him Plum because he looked like one, but in fact this chummy little name had been pressed into service by his family almost straight away as a simple contraction of his Christian name. Nonetheless, it may have been true that he looked like one. Another son was born to the Wodehouses, but not until eleven years later. After Plum, possibly a long run-up was felt to be necessary. Anyway, Richard Lancelot was born in 1892, the last of the romantically named Wodehouse offspring.

The first two years of P.G.'s life were spent *en famille* in Hong Kong, but then it was decided that a private – and English – education was necessary for all three Wodehouse boys. Their father, who had been educated at Repton, felt particularly strongly about this. The rather unfortunate and immediate effect of this decision, which, in the 1890s, was probably no decision at all, was that the family unit became split, and the boys had to settle down to a rather unusual childhood, seeing their parents only every seven years or so throughout the entire span of their schooldays. The reason for the infrequency of Ernest and Eleanor's visits to England is unclear, but this nonetheless was the pattern life assumed.

In 1884, a house was rented in Bath, where Eleanor had grown up. The three sons were left in the care of what seems to have been a miserable, humourless thing named Miss Roper, much possessed of all the traditionally dreary virtues such as scrupulous – if not fanatical – cleanliness, orderliness and formality. Just the sorts of things young lads relish. P.G. missed his parents, and missed what he felt real family life must be like, but as time advanced he came to see his mother only as an 'aunt' or 'friend of the family'. He did not suffer, though. He is on record as saying that he enjoyed his infancy greatly, seeing himself as in no way the victim of a 'broken home', or anything so dramatic. Indeed, he assured people later, it was this very enjoyment of his adolescence that precluded his ever being a great writer, for where, he wanted to know, was the pain? How could you be an artist if your father was 'as normal as rice pudding'? Irony was sizzling here, but critics have solemnly nodded in agreement. One influence this unusual upbringing might have had on his books, however, was the way in which he came to regard almost all older women as 'aunts', and hence was he free to appraise their good points, and translate their failings into humour. You can't laugh at mothers, decently. Even if your mother chews broken bottles and wears barbed wire next to the skin, it does not do to say so; rather do you excuse her as being highly-strung, or having been subject to a lot in her lifetime, or being prone to migraine, and then some. Aunts are just sufficiently removed, however, to allow you to let it rip. Aunts too can feel no qualms about lowering their gullible nephews into the thickest of soups, and enjoying every gurgle, though such actions would be unthinkable for Mater. But then of course, aunts aren't gentleman.

P.G. remained with the Roper for a couple of years, and in 1886 he and his brothers had a visit from their parents, whose arrival may or may not have had something to do with the fact that Ernest was to be invested as a C.M.G. by Queen Victoria, by virtue of the excellence of his work in Hong Kong. It was now time to move schools. Bath was exchanged for Croydon, but otherwise it appeared to be more of the same. The very small school was run by two spinster sisters – named Cissie and Florrie, I'm afraid – and these ladies too were very aware of what went to make the perfect little gentleman: liberal indulgence in all things tedious, and abstinence from anything remotely enjoyable, or even youthful. Much play was made of the boys being given a few pennies per week, on the strict understanding that they gave them away to those more deserving. In the eyes of small boys, there are no creatures on earth more deserving than themselves, and this went down rather hard. They were also taught to share anything good, but to hoard all the bad bits for themselves. Washing featured a good deal. All in all, they were being subjected to a 'good upbringing', and Wodehouse later admitted that a lot of it had actually worked, for he had been impressed by the importance of selflessness and consideration, though he regretted the fact that any form of adventure or fantasy was severely knocked on the head. There was no talk of fairies or make-believe; all was fact, Christianity and politeness. The two sisters were kind, however, and fair, if a little austere. P.G. remembers getting on well with the servants, possibly because of their less formal attitude to life. In his books, those below stairs are always painted as more warm and human, as are the more likeable gentlemen such as Emsworth, or Bertie. Except butlers, of course. P.G. never quite overcame his awe of butlers.

Life at Croydon chugged along, and true to the form of the best prodigies, P.G. was already at the age of seven, composing little stories. They were mainly quite poetic descriptions of the birds and trees he saw around him, Croydon yet being quite rural at the time. The brothers visited their grandmother every summer, and this delighted them. The delight, sad to record, was not due to the scintillating and irresistible company of the grandmother, however, who was not the chubby and story-telling old lady one might have expected. She was by now kindly, as were most of P.G.'s relatives, and she looked like a monkey. Plum tells us this. He was also quite surprised by the fact that his father had ever gained adulthood, for apparently this lady had pursued a minor career of thrashing him whenever she thought of it. Nonetheless, she seems to have simmered down into a fairly tolerant sort of chimp by the time her grandsons visited her, and she gave them the freedom of her very extensive home and grounds. It was this freedom which thrilled P.G. and his brothers, so great a contrast was it to life in Croydon. They visited her each summer for two weeks, and looked forward to it, you bet.

The pattern would probably have remained unchanged for some time, but for the fact that Peveril, son number one, had been diagnosed the possessor of a weak chest, the doctor concerned being of the opinion that Guernsey was the place to encourage weak chests to become less so. Although Peveril was some years older, and Armine had spent the earlier part of his childhood hitting Plum on the head whenever he had a spare moment, by this time a very strong friendship had developed between the three. A particular bond had formed between Armine and Plum, who was not sad to learn that the parents had decided that all three boys should go to Guernsey together, and start at another school. Ernest and Eleanor rather seemed to regard their offspring as the Three Musketeers by now, and pursued the attendant slogan with zeal, and even gusto.

In Guernsey, they attended a small public school not intended for boarders, and therefore the three lived with the headmaster, in his house. P.G. spent two years at Elizabeth College, which he seems to have enjoyed in a moderate sort of a way. The school he found merely 'pleasant', though he very much liked the Channel Islands themselves, and took great pleasure in exploring. The holidays were spent back in England with a miscellany of unsmiling aunts. There was never a shortage of aunts, though mirth did not seem to be their long suit. Later, P.G. reflected that it might have been his presence that made them so glum, and he toyed with the possibility that on the day he left, the aunt in question might be subject to quite uncontrolled delirium and joy, which would bubble relentlessly up until the moment when the blighted nephew was to make his return. The aunts must, he thought, be quite decent to put up with him at all.

At this point, for the first time, the Musketeers were to go their own ways. Peveril, whose chest was remaining obstinately below par, stayed on in Guernsey, and Armine was sent to Dulwich College in south London, seemingly for the reason that the boys' father had once passed through the town of Dulwich, and thought it a nice place.

For some reason, a little more thought seems to have gone into Plum's future, although this thought turned out to be rather misguided. It would appear logical and straightforward to have sent him along to Dulwich, together with Armine, particularly in view of the fondness the two had for each other, but Ernest was of the opinion that, for young Pelham, the thing to do was to plump for a Naval career, and hence the boy was dispatched to Malvern House, a Royal Navy preparatory school in Kent. Ernest's view was keenly supported by a clutch of aunts and uncles, indeed, everyone concerned or otherwise seemed convinced that the Navy was the thing for Plum. Except Plum.

He didn't like it. He didn't feel a part of it, and tended to go on long walks, alone. For the first time, it seemed that his schooldays had entered dry dock.

However, as in all the best school stories, help was at hand. A rosy, if not golden, future loomed. Plum visited Armine at Dulwich, and a very singular thing happened: he fell in love. With Dulwich College, that is. Most young boys would look at a school and be not too moved one way or another, but Plum was so utterly taken with everything about the place, that he pleaded with his father to be allowed to attend. The pleading must have been fairly strenuous, for he got his wish. It is possible that it was merely the contrast with his own school, at which he was unhappy, or that he was missing his brother's company, but the passion for Dulwich remained with him during his stay there, and throughout the rest of his life. Impossible as it may seem, it was an unusually enduring love affair with a school.

P. G. Wodehouse and *The Tie That Binds.*

CHAPTER TWO

JOY IN THE MORNING

There are few better things in life than a public school summer term. . . The freedom of it, after the restrictions of even the most easy-going private school, is intoxicating.

The brother of first-class cricketers has a dignity of his own.

MIKE

The 2nd of May, 1894. That was the day. Wodehouse, P.G., was starting at Dulwich, in the footsteps of his brother. Which was half the trouble. There was never any rivalry between Armine and Plum, it is true, but when your brother has already attended a school for two years, and has proved himself to be appallingly successful, it is not easy. At a boarding school, you simply did not come into contact with boys two years your senior, brothers or not. Consequently, Armine and Plum could only really pursue their friendship during the hols.

Straight away, P.G. was confronted with a situation where he had to live up to his brother's reputation. He was initially not to board in the school proper, but to live with one E. V. Doulton, a master who had a house in the town. The point was that Armine had also begun in this way, he and Doulton getting on splendidly. It is true that P.G. was beginning to prove the better sportsman of the two, but Armine was possessed of all the social graces and accomplishments, and Plum, he knew, was not. Worse, he didn't take to the wretched Doulton at all, but still had to live with the man for a term. P.G. was shy, and Armine was not. For the whole term P.G. felt he was being compared with big brother and being found wanting to the point of utter deficiency. Not that P.G. resented his brother for this; he was Armine's greatest fan. Nor was P.G. to prove a total failure in everything that Armine had excelled, indeed, with most things, such as editing the school magazine and making the 1st XI for cricket and the 1st XV for rugby, he followed on. But he followed on, that was the point.

A somewhat sullen Wodehouse in the Dulwich College 2nd XI, centre of the back row.

Some of which might lead one to think that when finally P.G. reached the school of his dreams, it was not all he had cracked it up to be. Not at all. He loved every minute – and even more so when at the beginning of the autumn term he was transferred to Ivyholme, one of the school houses where he boarded.

Meanwhile, in 1895, Plum's father was still in Hong Kong, busily contracting sunstroke. The sunstroke was no joke, and Ernest found himself retired from so demanding a post, though with a pension, a pension which, P.G. reminds us, was in rupees, not the most stable currency, and the main reason why he did not follow Armine to Oxford. Ernest and Eleanor now settled in Dulwich, together with the fourth Wodehouse boy, Richard Lancelot. His brothers called him Dick, for which he was doubtless profoundly grateful. The upshot of this move was that Armine and Plum ceased to be boarders and lived with their parents, virtually for the first time in their lives. Their father, it seemed, was an enthusiastic man, and they got on well with him, but Plum's attitude towards his mother was never really more than polite, possibly on account of the fact that he had only seen her two or three times during the past twelve years. He found her forbidding, and rather severe, but in Dulwich with his father and his brother, he didn't really mind that much. She had become one of the aunts.

This situation might have improved if only the Wodehouse parents had stayed put for two minutes. But no, by the end of the year family life seems to have palled, and they were off. They eventually settled in Shropshire, and Armine and Plum were boarders again.

By now, P.G. was fifteen, and still desperately shy. He was not good at small talk. He was not the life of the party. He dropped things. Perhaps because of these social shortcomings, he decided to devote himself to academic study, and try for an Oxford scholarship, as Armine had done. Not that he became a swot. There is a record that he still had time to invent a very stylish and grandiose variation of the game of conkers, whereby china chamber pots were dangled from adjacent high windows on a string, the two opponents undulating the cords with dexterity and panache in an attempt to induce upon the other's pot a state of smithereen. It is quite likely that the Dulwich authorities did not altogether approve of this game; two things are certain: they did not introduce the sport into the fixtures list, and soon after, all (remaining) ceramic pots were swopped for a more durable, if less cosy, metal.

Work was really the thing, though. His tutor turned out to be the blighted Doulton of three years earlier, but they seem to have bridged the gulf between their personalities by now and together they worked hard, and with results. In 1897 it was announced that Plum had gained the scholarship and could take his place at Oxford at the end of his Dulwich career. The problem was, as Armine had also gained a scholarship, the extra funds needed to finance both boys at Oxford were simply not forthcoming from Ernest's rupee-ridden stipend. Plum, being the minor, stood down.

The main buildings of Dulwich College.

Understandably, he did not now feel quite so enthusiastic about work as he had before, particularly when his father declared that Plum should pursue a life in the World of Commerce. This was a nonsense, for he had been following a classical education, and he neither knew nor cared even where the World of Commerce was situate. In Plum's view, the World of Commerce was a blight.

Partly by way of compensation, he redoubled his sporting efforts. Always keen, he now decided that this was the time for results. He was also now reading non-academic books, purely for pleasure, and had begun contributing pieces to the school magazine, *The Alleynian*. As with anything P.G. really put his mind to, all this bore fruit. Between 1897 and 1899, he had got into the 2nd XV rugger team, and the 2nd XI cricket. He was proficient, and gained Caps, but his failing eyesight was troubling him, particularly when he boxed. Though powerful physically, the weakness of his eyes meant that he was getting hit rather too often, which was annoying. However, he reached the 1st XV and 1st XI soon after, though, when Armine had gone on to Oxford, and he also became one of the editors of *The Alleynian*.

It is difficult to assess his expertise in sport with any accuracy, for P.G. regarded himself as having been only adequate, though with endless enthusiasm. Bill

1898	1899
KNOX F. P. *Capt.*	KRABBÉ C.F. *Capt.*
ANTHONY P.	WHITELEY L.A.
DOUGLAS S.M.	NIGHTINGALE F.L.
DOLBEY H.O.	FARQUHARSON J.C.L.
WODEHOUSE E.A.	HURLBATT D.G.
TREADGOLD J.R.W.	RIPLEY H.W.
CARMICHAEL D.W.W.	INGLIS A.L.
KRABBÉ C.F.	LEGG G.T.
COWES H.A.	GULLICK T.E.
BIRD G.R.	SKEY A.G.
SIME H.ST J.	WODEHOUSE P.G.

Townend, a contemporary at Dulwich, recalls his prowess thus: 'A noted athlete, a fine footballer and cricketer . . . in fact, one of the most important boys in the school.' A critique in *The Alleynian*, howsomever, goes like this:

'1st XV: A heavy forward. Has improved greatly, but is still inclined to slack in the scrum.

1st XI: Bowled well against Tonbridge, but did nothing else. Does not use his head at all. A poor bat and very slack field.'

Not kind stuff, but it was written by a fellow schoolboy. The point is, Plum enjoyed it all, and he continued to take great interest in Dulwich fixtures well into his old age.

It was now 1899, and Plum was doing disastrously in the Classical Sixth. He recalls that this didn't bother him overmuch, as he was getting on mightily with everyone and was particularly friendly with Bill Townend, with whom he shared a study. It was to Townend that Plum wrote all the letters in *Performing Flea*, and they were frantically loyal to each other throughout their lives. Townend became a writer, too, though never so successful as Plum, who often helped him out through the lean times, though discreetly and out of friendship, and not as 'the great man' scattering largesse. Wodehouse was never 'the great man'.

In 1900, P.G. left Dulwich, and in 1977 the school created a P.G. Wodehouse Corner in their library, in honour of their most famous Old Boy. His desk and swivel chair are there, as are his last typewriter, some books, pens, spectacles, pipes and tobacco pouches, a fitting memorial to one who loved the place so much. Amidst his praise of the school, though, P.G. once or twice had a stab at trying to classify its status. He described it as 'a middle-class school', though this was possibly intended not to convey the modern intimation of disgust. Raymond Chandler, who was also at Dulwich, agrees. He says it is 'not quite on the level of Eton and Harrow from a social point of view.' P.G. sums up: 'Bertie Wooster's parents would never have sent him to Dulwich.' So there.

His last term might have been a time for melancholy, particularly as he knew that his father had by now arranged for him a job in a bank, but something momentous happened. He wrote an essay called 'Some Aspects of Game Captaincy' which *The Public School Magazine* printed, and for which they paid a fee of half-a-guinea.

ABOVE LEFT: *At the bottom of the 1899 cricket side we see Plum.*
Ernest Armine is half way up the previous year, wouldn't you know it.

LEFT: *A Still-Life, taken in the P.G.W. Corner in the library of Dulwich College.*
The typewriter is not the original Monarch, but the later Royal electric.
The corn-cob pipe, the pouch and the spectacles are all P.G.'s, and the pencil reads:
'Half the Pressure, Twice the Speed.' Quite.

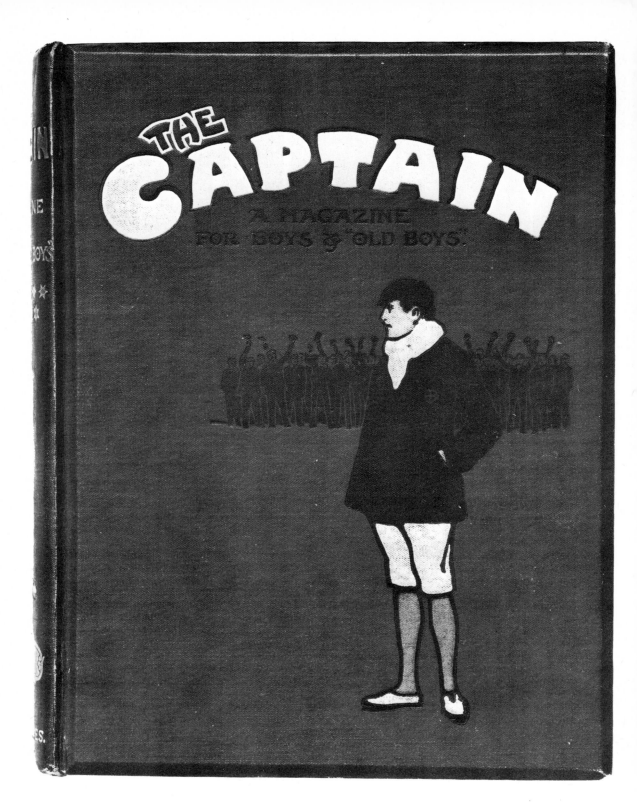

CHAPTER THREE

UNEASY MONEY

"Could you tell me," he said, "what I'm supposed to do? I've just joined the bank."

All this was very far removed from the life to which he had looked forward. There are some people who take naturally to a life of commerce. Mike was not of these. To him the restraint of the business was irksome. He had been used to an open-air life, and a life, in its way, of excitement. He gathered that he would not be free till five o'clock, and that on the following day he would come at ten and go at five, and the same every day, except Saturdays and Sundays, all the year round, with a ten days' holiday. The monotony of the prospect appalled him.

PSMITH IN THE CITY

Plum was now nineteen, and had told his father that he wanted to be a writer. Therefore, in the autumn of 1900, he took up his place in the Lombard Street branch of the Hong Kong and Shanghai Bank in London. His salary was £80 per year, and his father would match this sum with an allowance. P.G. was horrified by the whole caper, not least because he knew that the eventual idea was that one fine day he would be exported East to manage a whole new bank of his own, while, in his own words, he didn't feel up to managing a whelk-stall. However, his thorough classical education stood him in good stead when it came to sticking stamps on envelopes, which was all they would trust him with at first. P.G. accomplished the task with panache. It was only when the questions of Moneys, and Double-Entry and actual Banking came up that he began to quail. All the other young men employed by the bank seemed desperately keen and, worse, relatively competent. P.G. wished them luck, and burned the midnight oil. He wrote things. After a while, he had pieces accepted by such journals as *Tit-bits*, *St James's Gazette*, *Today* and *The Weekly Telegraph*, although his main efforts were still concentrated on *The Public School Magazine*. This magazine, owned by A. & C. Black, was becoming very popular, and possibly this fact alone prompted George Newnes to launch a rival, *The Captain*. And *The Captain* was willing to pay £3 for a story, which Plum decided, all in all, was a good thing. Although he continued to contribute to *The Public School Magazine*, notably with the serialization of what

The standard cover for a bound volume of The Captain.

would become his first published novel, *The Pothunters*, *The Captain* soon became his main outlet.

All this makes it sound very easy, and although it is true that P.G. never exactly found it difficult, and that during his two-year stint at the bank he had no less than eighty pieces printed in various periodicals, it is also true that his rejections numbered many hundreds. He sometimes wrote eight or ten stories in a week, and sent them everywhere. Most of them winged their way back. And, until *The Pothunters*, he himself regarded them all as pretty poor stuff; bilge is the word he selects to describe the bulk of it.

In 1901, he got mumps, and also a foot in the door of *The Globe* newspaper. The 'By the Way' column was edited, P.G. discovered, by an old Dulwich master, and he thought that he might approach him. The combination of Plum and The Old School Tie seemed to charm the birds off the trees, for he was offered the chance to do an occasional column, at half-a-guinea a time. This seemed to fit in very well with P.G.'s main project at the time, *The Pothunters*, commissioned by *The Public School Magazine*. In 1902, however, this periodical suddenly folded, but A. & C. Black, the parent company, promised to publish the novel in book form that year, at a 10% royalty.

Throughout all this heady stuff, P.G. was still at the bank, but not so as you'd notice. His heart was elsewhere, and so, according to the high-ups, was his mind. Wandering is the term. They seemed to share the view of his ex-headmaster, who regarded P.G. as a rather dithering and foolish boy, but likeable for all that. The banking hierarchy tolerated his presence and looked upon him, sometimes fondly, as their resident imbecile. In *Performing Flea*, P.G. tells us that due to his defacing a brand new ledger, Lombard Street decided that his likeability had plummetted to a new low and that his sanity had become seriously in question. The upshot was that The Hong Kong and Shanghai Bank confided in him that thenceforth they would do their best to struggle along alone, and unaided. The more likely reason for their parting company, although a parting was sooner or later inevitable, was that William Beach-Thomas, the ex-Dulwich master on *The Globe*, was about to splurge on a five-week holiday, and had offered P.G. the column for the duration. Plum, always a sprightly man, leapt. The bank men hid their grief as well as they could.

In writing, P.G. had discovered, in his own words, 'the only thing I thought I could do well', whereas banking – although the experience could not have been as disastrous as he implies, or he could never have sustained the two years – was simply not for him. Again, in his own words: 'I couldn't follow the thing at all. I didn't know what it was all about.'

The security of the bank was gone, and *The Globe* job was on for five weeks only. However, *The Pothunters* had now hit the bookstalls. His first book.

In his diary for the year, P.G. records the decision regarding the choice between *The Globe* and Commerce thus: 'I chucked the latter.' However, the five weeks

A signed presentation portrait of Plum, who seems only vaguely terrified.

passed, as weeks are prone to do, and soon he was without permanent employment. Determined now to be a writer, a good writer, and nothing but a writer, he resumed his bombardment of London's literary editors, this time succeeding with *Punch*, as well as with *The Evening News*, *Vanity Fair*, *The Captain* and others. His time was divided between his room in Walpole Street, Chelsea, and a Hampshire preparatory school where a recent acquaintance, Herbert W. Westbrook, was a resident master. In the village of Emsworth, actually, where P.G. later took a house called Threepwood.

Soon after, Beach-Thomas retired from *The Globe*, and P.G. got the 'By the Way' column for keeps, as he must have known he would. One of his first actions was to bring in Herbert Westbrook of Emsworth fame to act as his assistant. Although the column appeared six days a week, a collection of the things being published in 1908 (see Bibliography), P.G. was still turning out stories and articles for other journals at a fearful rate. There was, as they say, no stopping him. He had by now developed his talent for writing boys' stories that boys actually enjoyed reading and with which they could identify, and was expanding the themes into novels. It was now 1903, and A. & C. Black followed up *The Pothunters* with *A Prefect's Uncle* and also *St Austin's*, a collection of school stories which originally appeared in both *The Public School Magazine* and *The Captain*.

P.G., though, was no laurel rest-uponer. He was now working on the first novel for *The Captain*, *The Gold Bat*, which they would serialize over the months, and which was published in book form the following year. These early school books bear very little resemblance to later and mainstream Wodehouse, although humour and good-humour are there in abundance. Fags, uncles, prefects, tips, tuck and even bullies feature a deal, but the characters come over as pretty credible nonetheless, and are not nearly so black-and-white as those of, say, Frank Richards. Boys liked the stories, identified with the plots, and bought the magazine. Within the exclusive public school world of Captainites, then, Wodehouse became a name, and *The Gold Bat* put him into the (relatively) big money league, for it earned him £50. The books continued to be reprinted up to and through the War, and were reissued in a new format during the early twenties.

Possibly due to the £50, P.G. decided to more or less stick with *The Captain*. It was an amiably jingoistic magazine, aimed exclusively at public schoolboys, and edited by the Old Fag (R.S. Warren Bell, actually). It had a quite preposterous number of Corners for a merely rectangular journal. There were 'The Camera Corner', 'The Cycling Corner', 'The Athletics Corner', 'The Naturalists Corner', 'The Stamp Corner', and 'The Library Corner', among not a few other angles. In Volume Six, they even chuck in a story called 'The Tight Corner', for good, as it were, measure. Amongst the staple diet of school stories, there was a good deal of blood-and-thunder stuff, with titles like 'Mauled by a Tiger' and 'Famous Prison Escapes'. There were also 'Hints' on things like conjuring and, according to the

Index in one volume, 'Cigar Boxes, What To Do With, Old'. Presiding over all was the Old Fag himself, editing a sort of advice column for boys, rather like the back pages of the present womens' magazines, though without the naughty bits. His advice was fairly heavy-handed and pretty unhelpful. If a boy was worried about stammering or bat-ears, or some general sort of uselessness, he was instructed not to be. Be a man was the message. Be a 'Captainite'. Also available, to prove a chap's worth, was a badge. This cost sixpence, and was available either with pin, for lapel wear, or with eyelet, for use on watch-chain. The advertisements at the rear exhorted boys to Be Taller or Stop Giggling, simply by sending in the coupon below, together with some not-so-nominal remittance, and while they were at it, to buy five-shilling Ingersoll watches. W.G. Grace and G.A. Henty were regarded as just a short step only below God, and why not? Plum had found his audience.

In 1904, P.G. became eligible for *The Globe*'s five-week holiday, and he decided that America was the place to go. He had always been excited by the idea, though one of the main draws, believe it or not, was the American boxing scene, for he had retained his interest in the sport since Dulwich. He stayed on Fifth Avenue with someone he had known at the bank, proving that even boring jobs can have something to be said for them. He found New York, and the boxing, quite as thrilling as he had expected. Moreover, on returning from this binge, he found himself very much in demand as a journalist on the strength of having been transatlantic. He capitalized on it totally. Very soon he was deep into writing once more.

The Gold Bat – introducing Wrykyn, the school not at all loosely based on Dulwich – was published that year, as was *William Tell Told Again*, an untypical work, and simply a money-making retelling of the classic tale made to accompany Philip Dadd's illustrations, which were already in existence. And then he wrote his first song lyric. It was for the show *Sergeant Brue*, and he received five guineas for it.

By Christmas that year, P.G. was feeling pretty pleased with himself, so much so that he took the uncharacteristic step of chronicling his triumphs in his diary: '. . . I have *arrived*. I have a lyric in *Sergeant Brue*, a serial in *The Captain*, five books published, I am editing 'By The Way', *Pearson's* have two stories and two poems of mine, I have finished the Kid Brady stories, and I have a commission to do a weekly poem for *Vanity Fair*.'

True, all true. What, though, of a social life? Did this crammed calendar leave any space for friends? Women? That sort of thing? Well no, not really. By his own recollection, he used to go home from *The Globe*, and write. In the morning, he would come into *The Globe*, and write. However, despite the dearth of close relationships, Plum recalls: 'Well, I used to *know* a lot of girls and people.'

Ladykiller at large.

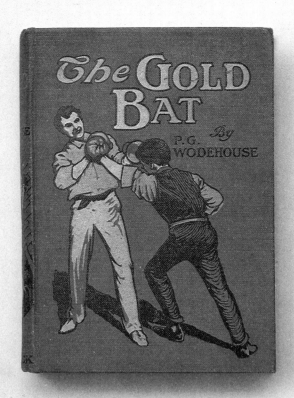

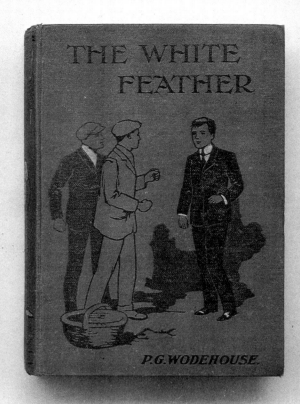

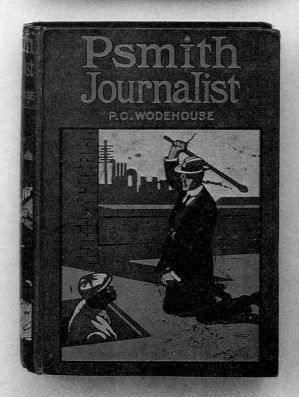

CHAPTER FOUR

SOMETHING FRESH

"Jeeves," I said, "you don't read a paper called Milady's Boudoir, do you?"
"No, sir. The periodical has not come to my notice."
"Well, spring sixpence on it next week, because this article will appear in it. Wooster on the Well Dressed Man, don't you know."
"Indeed, sir?"
"Yes, indeed, Jeeves. I've rather extended myself over this little bijou. There's a bit about socks that I think you will like."
He took the manuscript, brooded over it, and smiled a gentle, approving smile.
"The sock passage is quite in the proper vein, sir," he said.
"Well expressed, what?"
"Extremely, sir."

CARRY ON, JEEVES

There are signs now that despite P.G.'s success in the realm of boys' stories, he was beginning to be aware of their limitations. Or maybe he simply wished to write something different. Either way, this desire did not manifest itself immediately, and nor did P.G. see the advance into adult literature (which indicates something else now) as necessitating a break with the school stories. Indeed, in 1905, 'The White Feather' was being serialized in *The Captain*, and *The Head of Kay's* had been published in book form by Black. That summer, though, he got an adult story accepted by *The Strand*. Targets were very cut and dried in those days. *The Strand* was quite simply *the* magazine for stories, this status being largely due to Mr Sherlock Holmes who had ensured that each issue was a sell-out. Like *The Captain*, it was owned by Newnes.

This breakthrough was important, though so were the next couple of events, consolidating P.G.'s newly-sought status; he was now a 'proper' writer. Sir Seymour Hicks approached him, on the strength of his *Sergeant Brue* song, and commissioned a series of lyrics for future shows at The Aldwych, commencing with *The Beauty of Bath*. This second whiff of the theatre excited Plum very much, and he was impressed too by the young composer he was to work with, one Jerome Kern. The song they

Four early first editions, in their decorated bindings : The Gold Bat *(1904),*
The White Feather *(1907),* The Swoop *(1909), and* Psmith, Journalist *(1915).*

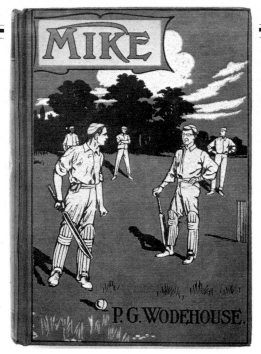

*The superb decorated binding of
the first edition of* Mike *(1909).*

first came up with – *Mr Chamberlain* – was, need it be said, a total success. P.G.'s future in musicals was already assured.

He must have grinned a fair deal around this time. He must have grinned while he worked. In 1906, he produced his first 'adult' novel, *Love Among the Chickens*, the plot suggested by a humorous anecdote related by Bill Townend in a letter, and concerning an acquaintance who had begun to raise chickens. The book was politely received, and netted Plum the sum of £31, £10 of which he characteristically sent to Townend. P.G. was fond of the book, though, and in 1920 it was reissued in a heavily revised form. The book is really notable for the introduction of Plum's pet character: Stanley Featherstonehaugh Ukridge.

Now, much play has been made of pronounciation here, so we may as well get it straight. This is mainly for people who make the first syllable of Wodehouse sound like that blue stuff with which primitive peoples used to daub themselves unsparingly. Ukridge is pronounced You-cridge. Featherstonehaugh is pronounced Fan-shaw, and Stanley, rather prosaically, is pronounced as in 'Dr Livingstone, I presume'. Anyway, the book was published by Newnes, and was also his first book to be published in America (see Bibliography).

P.G. worked on. In the next couple of years he produced, among other things, 'Junior Jackson' and 'The Lost Lambs' for *The Captain*, these two serials eventually being combined and published in book form as *Mike*. This saw the introduction of Mike, naturally enough, and also one of the great characters, Psmith (pronounced as W.H. Psmith & Son). Psmith wears a monocle, is eighteen, and rather wearied by life. The caption to one of the illustrations reads: 'Psmith seized and emptied Jellicoe's jug over Spiller', so you see he was very capable of fast-thinking action too. And you may depend on it, Spiller deserved it all, and more.

P.G. also published three rather untypical and unique works: *Not George Washington* (an adult novel again, though in collaboration with Herbert Westbrook),

P.G.'s only contribution to Chums *– 'The Luck Stone' by 'Basil Wyndham'
(actually Wodehouse and Townend).*

ONE AIRSHIP AGAINST A FLEET.

See Our Thrilling War Serial by Capt. Shaw on page 66..

CHUMS

THE LUCK STONE.

A Splendid School Serial crammed with Fun and Adventure (see page 71).

No. 839.—Vol. XVII.] OCTOBER 7, 1908. PRICE ONE PENNY.

A CLASS-ROOM INDIGNATION MEETING.

When Jimmy and Tommy entered the room order had been restored to a certain extent.

(You will find the names of everyone of these amusing chums mentioned in our splendid school serial on page 71.)

Wodehouse in 1928, sitting in, rather than driving, a shimmering AC.
The nearest he ever came to being Wooster.

The Globe By the Way Book – a little paperback culling from the column, again written with Westbrook – and *The Swoop*, another paperback, and rather strange in most ways. It is a cautionary tale with humour, subtitled *How Clarence Saved England*, and it was written in five days flat.

He was still working on *The Globe*, but the general feel in the air seemed to be Onward, Yes, and ever Upward. Progress was the word, and a second trip to America loomed large. One of the reasons for the projected trip was that his agent over there, one Baerman, had sold the serial rights of *Love Among the Chickens* for some fairly dizzying sum, but seemed strangely loath to actually pass any of the folding stuff in Plum's direction. A thousand dollars was the sum, and P.G. could hardly wait to get hold of it. Baerman didn't seem to be in the same sort of hurry, however, and stalled for months. A cheque eventually did arrive, it is true, but P.G. was not slow to see that it was quite unsigned. This was a taste of the 'business world', and Plum later saw this little alliance with Baerman as 'the making of him'. After a while, dribs of money filtered through, and then the periodic drab. However, it was not the way business ought to be conducted, though years later, P.G. was of the opinion that for a slightly increased insight into Life, he was much in Baerman's debt; Baerman for his part still owed him $200. At the time, it all had to be seen to, but it was really only an excuse for the New York trip, rather than the reason.

Even before he left, things were fizzing quite nicely. In 1906, Sir Seymour Hicks had made P.G. his chief lyricist, but the following year they parted company, Plum signing up with The Gaiety. There was no animosity, of course; indeed, they had become quite close friends. So trusting was Wodehouse that he even bought a used car from the man, for roughly most of the money he had in the world. Plum was well pleased, though. He aimed the motor at the village Emsworth, but quite early on in the proceedings he contrived to hit a large and unyielding hedge, not very much less than forcibly. He never drove again.

CHAPTER FIVE

THE MATING SEASON

In New York you may find every class of paper which the imagination can conceive. Every grade of society is catered for. If an Esquimau came to New York, the first thing he would find on the bookstalls in all probability would be the 'Blubber Magazine', or some similar production written by Esquimaux for Esquimaux. Every-body reads in New York, and reads all the time.

PSMITH, JOURNALIST

She got right in amongst me. Her beauty maddened me like wine. . . In New York, I have always found, one gets off the mark quickly in matters of the heart. This, I believe, is due to something in the air.

THANK YOU, JEEVES

And in 1909, P.G. was in New York again, in Greenwich Village this time. He secured a new agent who straightaway sold two of his stories, for $500. This fast and lucrative transaction inspirited P.G. most frantically. There was no doubt about it, he felt sure: New York *was* the place to be. There were hundreds of magazines around, and all seemed potential markets; also, America being America, they paid better. One feels that Plum might have rather too deeply inhaled the Manhattan air, for very soon he was cabling his resignation to *The Globe* in London, and planning on prolonging his stay in New York indefinitely. And he bought a typewriter to settle the thing.

It wasn't to be like that, though. It transpired that in America, things were done a little differently. They did not want to commission serials, as did *The Captain* in London, but only one-offs; and they were pretty choosy. Neither, of course, did he have a regular job. But did this bother Plum? Well, yes it did, rather, so he returned to England and bought Threepwood, the house in Emsworth which he had formerly been renting, and seems to have had not the slightest trouble in resuming his post at *The Globe*. He really must have been damnably likeable. And, of course, good.

Over the next three or four years, Plum wrote on. He hardly did anything else, dividing his time between *The Globe* offices, Threepwood – into which he had imported his American typewriter, and a plurality of dogs – and New York. In his own words, he 'sort of shuttled to and fro' quite a deal. His stories were almost all published by *The Strand* at this time, though novels were coming out too, *Psmith in the City*, drawing on P.G.'s experiences in Lombard Street, and, perhaps more notably, *A Gentleman of Leisure*. This is the first book that is the sort of thing people mean when they talk of 'a Wodehouse novel'. All the ingredients are there: country houses, silly aristocrats, and even sillier young things. There is also, few will be surprised to hear, a butler — one Saunders, by name. Quite a few avid readers are unaware of the existence of the school stories, and would be a little disappointed by such works as *William Tell Told Again* or *The Globe By the Way Book*. They know what they want — romantic humour, liberally peppered with Eggs, Beans, Crumpets, Drones, Peers, Aunts and Butlers. Ten-year-olds love them, and old men and women have been known to die in an ecstasy of loving them. They bridge all gaps — generation, class and

A typical Strand *cover, with Wodehouse out-ranking the mighty Conan Doyle.*

race. It seems strange, on the face of it; they ought not to, really, but that is the way. Deathless is the word, and *A Gentleman of Leisure* was the first. On one of his transatlantic trips, Plum was asked to make a play of it, and he said why not? It opened on Broadway in 1911, with Douglas Fairbanks Senior in the leading role.

Things were popping, and they continued to pop in more ways than one. In America, Munsey's Magazine had commissioned *The Little Nugget*, and Plum was also writing stories for *Vanity Fair*, quite a few of them pseudonymously. In England, he was collaborating on a revue, *Nuts and Wine*, with Charles Bovill.

Plum was living in London now, having finally decided that a country residence, no matter how pleasant or humble, was not the way of an urban scribe. Stories continued to flow from the pen, and a collection, *The Man Upstairs*, was published in 1914.

But what of the fair sex? Not much, so far. Plum's New York and London were not the night-life capitals of the world. The night was a time for writing – and so, for that matter, was the day. But even hard workers like P.G. can make the time if the opportunity arises, and in New York in the summer of 1914, it did. He was introduced to a young widow named Mrs Rowley. She was English, and Plum liked her. He called her Ethel, for this was her name.

The day after their meeting saw the outbreak of the First World War, but one receives the distinct impression that Plum hardly noticed. It seemed rather unimportant when compared with his feelings for this girl. She was four years younger than he, had married at the age of eighteen, and had a nine-year old daughter, Leonora, who was boarding in England. Her husband had died of an infection in India.

The two spent their days on Long Island, and romance blossomed. It positively burgeoned. One imagines the head swimming, and Plum clutching at the odd passing table. This was the real thing all right. Money, however, was low. Despite being up to his ears in passion, then, he still wrote on in the evenings, mainly for *Vanity Fair*. Proper aid came from Munsey's, however, who at this most auspicious moment chose to pay him his first really handsome fee for *The Coming of Bill* – $2000.

Just a couple of months later, Plum decided that the time had come to pop the question, not to say take the plunge. He never was the greatest person at handling speeches and declarations, however, and he recalls that this occasion was no exception. He sneezed a lot, it seems, and Mrs Rowley, though taken with the man, could quite frankly take his germs or leave them. Nonetheless she went along with the idea and soon the deed was done. Mr and Mrs Wodehouse took an apartment in New York, and rented a smaller place on their beloved Long Island.

Plum also tried to enlist in the Army a few times about now, but they didn't want him. His eyes, they said, were very weak. He had become used to this sort of thing, however, so he soon got over the blow. His thoughts turned once more to his career, for with this young woman at his side he felt that there was really nothing he could not achieve. Short-sighted, maybe, but he jolly well did have vision.

THE SATURDAY EVENING POST

An Illu Weekly
Founded A . Franklin

JUNE 26, 1915   5c. THE COPY

Beginning
Something New—By Pelham Grenville Wodehouse

CHAPTER SIX

BRING ON THE GIRLS

Three days after that Egbert arrived at Evangeline's flat with tickets for the theatre.
"I am sorry –" began Evangeline.
"Don't say it," said Egbert. "Let me guess. You are going to the theatre with Mr. Banks?"
"Yes, I am. He has seats for the first night of Tchekhov's 'Six Corpses in Search of an Undertaker'."
"He has, has he?"
"Yes, he has."
"He has, eh?"
"Yes, he has."

'Best Seller' from MULLINER NIGHTS

A short time earlier, Plum had made Ella King-Hall his English agent, at a time when this lady had just become Herbert Westbrook's wife; P.G. was never one to forget a friendship. In America too, now, he transferred to one Paul Reynolds. This was the beginning of the big money, for Reynolds managed to sell Plum's new serial 'Something New' to *The Saturday Evening Post*. For $3500.

The Saturday Evening Post was the magazine to end them all. They paid very well indeed and the prestige was enormous. The top names were published here, and top artists illustrated the work and furnished the covers. The magazine was edited by George Lorimer, who personally read every major contribution and judged the work purely on its merit, regardless of the fame of the author or of any personal relationship that might exist between the two. Hence the prestige, and hence the magazine's consistent quality. Lorimer also accepted *Uneasy Money*, though we don't know whether this title had anything remotely to do with the fact that this time the fee was upped to a rounded $5000.

Neither, of course, had Plum neglected *Vanity Fair*, which now appointed him Drama Critic. It is difficult to understand quite why *Vanity Fair* should have felt so moved, but P.G., yet retaining his fascination for the grease-paint, accepted with a bound. At least it got him out of the house.

However, however. As with many other chance happenings in Plum's life, this appointment was to have its reverberations. His first assignment was to cover *Very*

A Saturday Evening Post *cover, the damsel well into the new Wodehouse novel.*

Good, Eddie, which Plum thought very good, really, and backstage he re-encountered Jerome Kern, who had written the music, and – for the first time – Guy Bolton, the author of the book. Kern, of course, P.G. knew and liked from his earlier collaboration, and Guy Bolton he seemed to take to immediately. All three agreed that *Very Good, Eddie* was a welcome departure from the usual sort of Broadway musical, which ran to a formula of a weak-to-dying story line, interspersed with as much pizazz as possible. Neither Bolton nor Kern was really happy with the lyrics,

The composer and song-writer Jerome Kern in 1928.

however. Indeed, as Bolton reports in *Bring on the Girls*, Kern was rather dissatisfied with the state of American lyrics in general. He quotes the following few as an example, the exclusion of which, he felt, could only improve a show: "Give me your hand. You'll understand. We're off to Slumberland." These, if you like, from *Babes in the Wood*.

P.G., Kern knew, was the last word in lyricists, and consequently the triumvirate was formed almost before the words were spoken. The Kern-Bolton-Wodehouse team was on the air, and almost immediately the commissions came in, notably from Abraham Erlanger who owned most of the best New York theatres. In partnership with one Marc Klaw, actually.

It was summer 1916, and P.G. was working with Guy and Jerome on *Miss Springtime*, as well as on a new serial, Piccadilly Jim. His stepdaughter now made her second visit to the Wodehouse home, and Plum welcomed this enormously, for at their first meeting the previous year they had hit it off most utterly. Already, Leonora was becoming one of the best things in Plum's life. Somehow, he managed to juggle all these goings-on, and sold Piccadilly Jim to *The Saturday Evening Post* for $7500. Almost immediately, he embarked upon a new musical comedy with Kern and Bolton, *Have a Heart*.

Miss Springtime opened and was a success. All the critics said it was a success, including P.G. Wodehouse, who reviewed it for *Vanity Fair*.

It all came pretty thick and fast after that, P.G. devoting nearly all of his energies into this new-found and highly successful medium. *Have a Heart* went well and soon the three were hard at work on *Oh, Boy!*, which turned out to be Broadway's greatest hit of the season, running for about a year-and-a-half. Bolton and Wodehouse had become America's most sought-after musical comedy authors.

The next major undertaking was a revue, commissioned by Flo Ziegfeld. Not just a revue, but a Revue, for Ziegfeld seemed determined upon the hit of the century. It was to be called *Miss 1917*, and an absolutely AI cast had been assembled. Kern Bolton and Wodehouse set to. The rehearsal pianist, it is interesting to note, was called George Gershwin, happy to be earning $30 per week in his first professional job. Eventually, at vast expense and to a positive fanfare of publicity, the show opened. It was a complete flop and lost a fortune. It's a funny thing, the stage.

The great George Gershwin in 1928, aged thirty.

They were all a bit miffed, but undeterred. *Oh, Lady! Lady!* was the next, and this turned out to be quite a smash. The *Vanity Fair* review said: 'Bolton and Wodehouse and Kern are my favourite indoor sport.' But one is gratified to know that P.G. had given up the column by now, and that this was written by Dorothy Parker.

Plum began to move around a little. He and Ethel took a house in London for a while, in order to visit Leonora at school. Frances – now Lady – Donaldson, a fellow pupil, tells us that once P.G. was spotted crouching behind some bushes in an effort to avoid an encounter with the headmistress,

THE PLAY

PICTORIAL

With which are incorporated
"THE PLAY," "THE PLAY SOUVENIR," "THE STAGE SOUVENIR"

"KISSING TIME"

NO. 207

VOL. XXXIV

1 S. NET

MONTHLY

MISS PHYLLIS DARE
MR. GEORGE GROSSMITH

who quite frankly terrified the life out of him.

P.G. and Ethel also went on a holiday to Palm Beach, and Guy Bolton came along. If it was leisure they were after, or the complete and bracing change, they didn't quite attain it, for who should they run into but Florenz Ziegfeld, who cabled Jerome Kern to join them all on his yacht. He wanted, he said, to discuss a new show. To Ziegfeld, holidays had to have some point, or else what was the point?

The Wodehouses were now permanently based in Great Neck, Long Island, and it was here that most of Plum's writing was done. It is true that he had not produced nearly so much fiction as formerly – as was inevitable, due to his very heavy musical commitments – but one book was published in 1917, *The Man with Two Left Feet*. Although only a volume of stories previously published in magazines, it is very notable for one in particular: 'Extricating Young Gussie'. On the opening page of this, the following line of dialogue appears:

'Mrs Gregson to see you, sir.'

Unremarkable in itself, perhaps, but it does happen to be spoken by Jeeves, to the young master Bertie. We have never met them before, but they come up again.

Plum liked life at Great Neck. He says: 'The golf course was awfully nice. However, I wasn't any good at golf . . . but then I hadn't really much time for doing anything because I was writing all the time.'

A 1919 cover of The Play, *showing a still*
from the London production of Kissing Time.
Plum had 'anglicized' the American The Girl Behind the Gun.

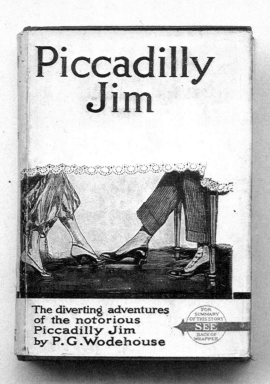

Piccadilly Jim

The diverting adventures of the notorious Piccadilly Jim by P. G. Wodehouse

FOR SUMMARY OF THIS STORY SEE BACK OF WRAPPER

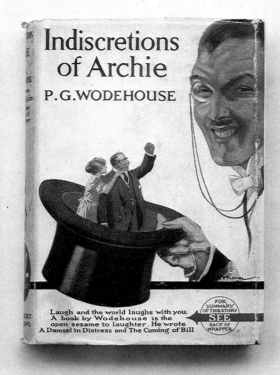

Indiscretions of Archie
P. G. WODEHOUSE

Laugh and the world laughs with you. A book by Wodehouse is the open sesame to laughter. He wrote A Damsel in Distress and The Coming of Bill

FOR SUMMARY OF THIS STORY SEE BACK OF WRAPPER

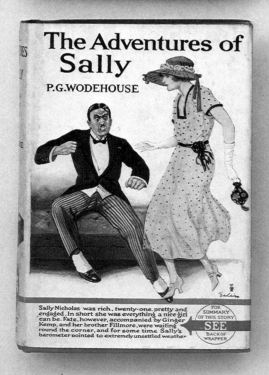

The Adventures of Sally
P. G. WODEHOUSE

Sally Nicholas was rich, twenty-one, pretty and engaged. In short she was everything a nice girl can be. Fate, however, accompanied by Ginger Kemp, and her brother Fillmore, were waiting round the corner, and for some time Sally's barometer pointed to extremely unsettled weather

FOR SUMMARY OF THIS STORY SEE BACK OF WRAPPER

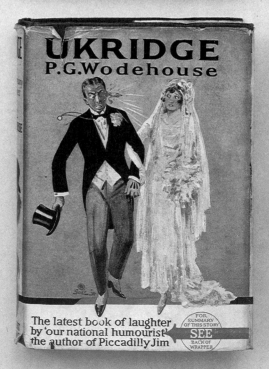

UKRIDGE
P. G. Wodehouse

The latest book of laughter by 'our national humourist' the author of Piccadilly Jim

FOR SUMMARY OF THIS STORY SEE BACK OF WRAPPER

CHAPTER SEVEN

PERFORMING FLEA

"My nephew has probably told you that I have been making a close study of your books of late?"
he began.
"Yes. He did mention it. How – er – how did you like the bally things?"
"Mr. Wooster, I am not ashamed to say that the tears came into my eyes as I listened to them.
It amazes me that a man as young as you can have been able to plumb human nature so surely to its depth;
to play with so unnerring a hand on the quivering heart-strings of your reader; to write novels so true,
so human, so moving, so vital!"
"Oh, it's just a knack," I said.
The good old persp. was bedewing my forehead by this time in a pretty lavish manner. I don't know when
I've been so rattled.

THE INIMITABLE JEEVES

"Women," commented the Biscuit, "ought never to be allowed cheque-books. I've often said so."

BIG MONEY

In 1920, P.G. wrote to Bill Townend, his old school friend, recounting *The Saturday Evening Post* successes, and passing on the news of his latest sale, *A Damsel in Distress*, for $10,000 – adding: 'So now I can afford an occasional meat meal, not only for self but for wife and resident kitten and bulldog.' He also talked about his current projects: a serial for Collier's (Jill the Reckless) and The Girl on the Boat – 'for, if you'll believe it, *The Woman's Home Companion*. Heaven knows what a women's magazine wants with my sort of stuff.' But after all, they were paying $15,000 for it. P.G. mentions casually at the end of his letter that he was toying also with some more stories for *The Saturday Evening Post* 'about a bloke called Bertie Wooster and his valet'.

The stories would not appear in book form for some years – as *The Inimitable Jeeves* – though in 1919 a Jeeves book had already been published. Called *My Man Jeeves*, it was a small, cheap-looking volume of stories, only half of which concerned Jeeves, published as part of a series by Newnes (see Bibliography). Possibly because it did not really seem a volume to reckon with, very little notice of it was taken.

Four first editions: Piccadilly Jim *(1918),* Indiscretions of Archie *(1921),*
The Adventures of Sally *(1922), and* Ukridge *(1924).*

Although P.G. was still very much concerned with the theatre, and the alliance with Kern and Bolton was as strong as ever, he was devoting more time now to fiction, and in another letter to Townend he gives us a glimpse of how he worked.

> I now write stories at terrific speed. I've started a habit of rushing them through and then working over them very carefully, instead of trying to get the first draft exactly right, and have just finished the rough draft of an 8000-word story in two days.

He had the goodness to add, 'It nearly slew me', and goes on, 'As a rule, I find a week long enough for a short story, if I have the plot well thought out. On a novel I generally do eight pages a day, i.e. about 2500 words.'

The world of theatre was creeping into his novels now, as was inevitable from his absorption, and also from his golden dictum that he would never set a book in a world he did not understand. The plot of *A Damsel in Distress* bears this out. The structure of theatre was evident not only in the very tight entrances and exits, but in the way the story was split into scenes with 'as little stuff between the scenes as possible.' It was, in short, all good bits. This approach, thought Plum, was 'based on an instinctive knowledge of stagecraft'. P.G.'s first draft he would refer to as the 'scenario'; the plot and structure was all at the beginning. This would then be fleshed out into an enormously long novel which would eventually undergo ruthless pruning and polishing. In another letter to Townend, Plum passes on the following gem. 'I suppose the secret of writing is to go through your stuff till you come on something you think is particularly good, and then cut it out.'

It really is quite incredible that he had the time to write letters at all, but he did, and quite a few. But then, so did all the great writers. As soon as the rather forbidding *Collected Letters Of* . . . start appearing, it becomes clear that what in fact those great w.'s did was merely slip in the odd deathless work between the chatty correspondence which was the mainstay of their lives.

Plum, in his mid-forties, at work with his beloved Monarch typewriter.

While this was not quite the case with Plum, he fairly burned the notepaper, most of it ending up with Bill Townend, though a good deal was also written to his now totally adored step-daughter, Leonora. Their relationship was clearly just what the doctor ordered, as may be seen from the openers and closers of a typical letter: 'Darling Snorkles . . . well, cheerio, old fright. Write again soon. Your loving Plummie.' Rather pre-empts Bertie and his Aunt Dahlia, don't you know.

And not only letter-writing, but reading. P.G. had always read a lot as a matter of course – old favourites, as diverse as Shakespeare and Conan Doyle – and also the latest fiction. One such work that greatly impressed him was Denis Mackail's *What Next?*, so much so that he wrote to the author in its praise and dined him at The Savoy Grill. A strong and, needless to say, lifelong relationship sprang out of this, with affection and respect on both sides. This is exemplified in P.G.'s dedication in *Summer Lightning*, nine years on: 'To Denis Mackail, author of *Greenery St, The Flower Show and Other Books Which I Wish I Had Written*.' Of the inaugural dinner, Mackail tells us in *Life With Topsy* that Wodehouse immediately started talking about writing. 'For this – apart from Pekes, and cricket and football matches at his old school, with which he also seemed obsessed – was his own, great, unending topic.'

Around this time Plum and Ethel took a brief trip to America, he writing furiously throughout both journeys, as well as during their stay. He was working both on a novel, and on the lyrics for another show, *The Golden Moth*, this time with music by Ivor Novello. It was a fairly enjoyable if hard-working trip, though the Wodehouses' main purpose had been to sell the house in the Great Neck, which they did. The Prohibition was on at the time, though apparently Scotch was available if you had the seventeen necessary dollars. This, in 1921.

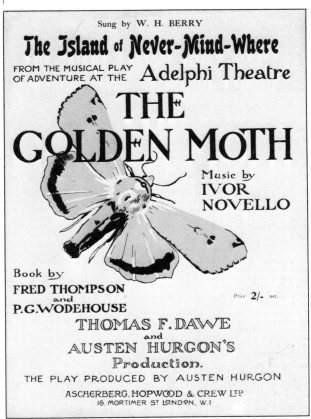

Sheet music from the Novello/Wodehouse collaboration.

On their return, Ethel bought a racehorse, which must have seemed a fairly sound idea at the time. It made a change from groceries. Nevertheless, it turned out to be quite a good move, as it actually won races. Which was just as well, as Ethel tended to back it to the hilt.

The Golden Moth was proving successful, and now its star, George Grossmith, wondered whether P.G. and Jerome Kern were interested in collaborating on yet another show. They were. All three set sail for New York, planning the thing during the voyage. It was a productive trip and P.G. wrote a good deal on the ship. In fact, everything was pretty rosy until he was asked to perform at the ship's concert. Gloom descended upon the hitherto sunny brow. Plum was not a performer. He wasn't good at it. It was not, he considered, his style; indeed – he was still fairly prone to dropping things. Eventually he decided that a reading from his latest work would prove the least painful task, and so he proceeded to screw the courage. But even with oratory, P.G. had his short-comings: he was no orator. He began at page one in a wacky sort of a mumble, and carried on droning into the night. Now it possibly would not have been so bad if his audience could have heard him, or if he had not been the last on the bill. But this was not the case, and the said audience grew restless. A little later, they pushed off altogether. Plum didn't mind at all, as he was just beginning to get into the swing of the thing. Make it snappy, had been Grossmith's advice, but Plum maybe hadn't heard. The ballroom was empty, the lights were dimmed, and Plum drivelled on delightedly. This anecdote has been reconstructed from Grossmith's possibly coloured retelling of the incident. Or possibly not.

Anyway, the result of this latest collaboration was *Cabaret Girl*, which made its debut in September 1922. It was a success, of course, but by that time P.G. was

The original caption to this photograph taken in the late twenties reads :
'Irving Berlin, Jewish emigrant boy who worked his way up to the nation's
most popular song-writer, with his bride, the former Ellen McKay,
daughter of the millionaire president of the Postal Telegraph Co.'

already working on another, this time with Guy Bolton and Irving Berlin. As to his latest novel, he wrote the following to Townend: 'The Saturday Evening Post has done me proud. Although they never commission anything, they liked the first 60,000 words of Leave it to Psmith so much that they announced it in the papers before I sent in the remainder. I mailed them the last part on a Wednesday and got a cheque for $20,000 on the following Tuesday.' But then, are not all authors familiar with such munificence and promptitude?

The Wodehouses were now either on Long Island, or in London. They had a house rented in each location, though they tended to spend the summers in America, when Leonora would join them. She and her mother would entertain guests and visitors, while Plum would slope off and write, whenever he got the chance. Ethel loved society, not to say Society, but P.G., although he liked and needed the company of his (very few) real friends, did not have a lot of interest in guests, visitors and acquaintances. His lack of small talk came into this, but the main factor was time itself; there was so much to do.

Herbert Jenkins published The Inimitable Jeeves, and the gentleman's gentleman (not valet, as P.G. had initially seen him) made a very distinct impression indeed. The Kern-Wodehouse-Grossmith show had just opened, and P.G. had prepared Leave it to Psmith for book publication. In the blurb, the appearance of another Psmith story was blamed on Leonora.

Psmith – the p is silent as in pshrimp – was the hero of a book for boys which I wrote in the year 1909 when I was young and slim and had quite a crop of hair. I had always intended some day to write of his after-school life, but never quite got down to it till my golden-haired child, who is the world's worst pest, harried me day by day in every way to such an extent that I saw the thing had to be done. So I did it.

And the dedication ran: 'To My Daughter Leonora, Queen of her Species.' She must have continued to be the world's worst pest too, for a couple of years later P.G. dedicates The Heart of a Goof to her thus: 'To My Daughter Leonora, Without Whose Never Failing Sympathy and Encouragement This Book Would Have Been Finished In Half The Time.' Familist authors know the feeling.

It was a full life, though, what with one thing and another. A letter to Townend begins: 'Have you ever been knocked over by a car? If not, don't. There's no percentage in it.' He goes on to describe a recent encounter with a Ford.

I suddenly observed with interest that it wasn't stopping but was swinging in straight for me on the wrong side of the road. I gave one gazelle-like spring sideways and the damned thing's right front wheel caught my left leg squarely and I thought the world had ended. I took the most awful toss and came down on the right side of my face and skinned my nose, my left leg and my right arm.

BUTTERCUP DAY

By P. G. Wodehouse

ILLUSTRATED BY MAY WILSON PRESTON

"LADDIE," said Ukridge, "I need capital, old horse—need it sorely."

He removed his glistening silk hat, looked at it in a puzzled way and replaced it on his head. We had met by chance near the eastern end of Piccadilly, and the breathtaking gorgeousness of his costume told me that since I had seen him last there must have occurred between him and his Aunt Julia one of those periodical reconciliations which were wont to punctuate his hectic and disreputable career. For those who know Stanley Featherstonehaugh Ukridge, that much-enduring man, are aware that he is the nephew of Miss Julia Ukridge, the wealthy and popular novelist; and that from time to time, when she can bring herself to forgive and let bygones be bygones, he goes to dwell for a while in gilded servitude at her house in Wimbledon.

"Yes, Corky, my boy, I want a bit of capital."

"Oh?"

"And want it quick. The truest saying in this world is that you can't accumulate if you don't speculate. But how the deuce are you to start speculating unless you accumulate a few quid to begin with?"

"Ah," I said, noncommittally.

"Take my case," proceeded Ukridge, running a large, beautifully gloved finger round the inside of a spotless collar which appeared to fit a trifle too snugly to the neck. "I have an absolutely safe double for Kempton Park on the fifteenth, and even a modest investment would bring me in several hundred pounds. But bookies, blast them, require cash down in advance, so where am I? Without capital, enterprise is strangled at birth."

"Can't you get some from your Aunt Julia?" I asked him.

"Not a cent. She is one of those women who simply do not disgorge. All her surplus cash is devoted to adding to her collection of moldy snuffboxes. When I look at those snuffboxes and reflect that any single one of them, judiciously put up the spout, would set my feet on the road to fortune, only my innate sense of honesty keeps me from pinching them."

"You mean they're locked up."

"It's hard, laddie; very hard and bitter and ironical. She buys me suits, she buys me hats, she buys me boots, she buys me spats; and, what is more, insists on my wearing the damned things. With what result? Not only am I infernally uncomfortable but my exterior creates a totally false impression in the minds of any blokes I meet to whom I may happen to owe a bit of money. When I go about looking as if I owned the mint, it becomes difficult to convince them that I am not in a position to pay them their beastly one pound fourteen and eleven or whatever it is. I tell you, laddie, the strain has begun to weigh upon me to such an extent that the breaking point may arrive at any moment. Every day it is becoming more imperative that I clear out and start life again upon my own. But this cannot be done without cash. And that is why I look around me and say to myself, 'How am I to acquire a bit of capital?'"

"Buttercup Day," She Said Winningly

I thought it best to observe at this point that my own circumstances were extremely straitened. Ukridge received the information with a sad, indulgent smile.

"I was not dreaming of biting your ear, old horse," he said. "What I require is something far beyond your power to supply. Five pounds at least—or three, anyway. Of course, if, before we part, you think fit to hand over a couple of bob or half a crown as a small temporary ——"

He broke off with a start, and there came into his face the look of one who has perceived snakes in his path. He gazed along the street; then, wheeling round, hurried abruptly down Church Place.

"One of your creditors?" I asked.

"Girl with flags," said Ukridge briefly. A peevish note crept into his voice. "This modern practice, laddie, of allowing females with trays of flags and collecting boxes to flood the metropolis is developing into a scourge. If it isn't Rose Day it's Daisy Day, and if it isn't Daisy Day it's Pansy Day. And though now, thanks to a bit of quick thinking, we have managed to escape without ——"

At this moment a second flag girl, emerging from Jermyn Street, held us up with a brilliant smile, and we gave till it hurt—which, in Ukridge's case, was almost immediately.

"And so it goes on," he said bitterly. "Sixpence here, a shilling there. Only last Friday I was touched for twopence at my very door. How can a man amass a huge fortune if there is this constant drain on his resources? What was that girl collecting for?"

"I didn't notice."

"Nor did I. One never does. For all we know, we may have contributed to some cause of which we heartily disapprove. And that reminds me, Corky, my aunt is lending her grounds on Tuesday for a bazaar in aid of the local

temperance league. I particularly wish you to put aside all other engagements and roll up."

"No, thanks; I don't want to meet your aunt again."

"You won't meet her. She will be away. She's going north on a lecturing tour."

"Well, I don't want to come to any bazaar. I can't afford it."

"Have no fear, laddie. There will be no expense involved. You will pass the entire afternoon in the house with me. My aunt, though she couldn't get out of lending these people her grounds, is scared that, with so many strangers prowling about, somebody might edge in and sneak her snuffboxes. So I am left on guard, with instructions not to stir out till they've all gone—and a very wise precaution too. There is absolutely nothing which blokes whose passions have been inflamed by constant ginger beer will stick at. You will share my vigil. We will smoke a pipe or two in the study, talk of this and that; and it may be that, if we put our heads together, we shall be able to think up some sort of scheme for collecting a bit of capital."

"Oh, well, in that case ——"

"I shall rely on you. And now, if I don't want to be late I'd better be getting along. I'm lunching with my aunt at Prince's."

He gazed malevolently at the flag girl, who had just stopped another pedestrian, and strode off.

Heath House, Wimbledon, the residence of Miss Julia Ukridge, was one of that row of large mansions which face the common, standing back from the road in the seclusion of spacious grounds. On any normal day the prevailing note of the place would have been a dignified calm; but when I arrived on the Tuesday afternoon a vast unusual activity was in progress. Over the gates there hung large banners advertising the bazaar, and through these gates crowds of people were passing. From somewhere in the interior of the garden came the brassy music of a merry-go-round.

I added myself to the throng, and was making for the front door when a silvery voice spoke in my ear, and I was aware of a very pretty girl at my elbow.

"Buy a buttercup?"

"I beg your pardon?"

"Buy a buttercup?"

I then perceived that, attached to her person with a strap, she carried a tray containing a mass of yellow paper objects.

"What's all this?" I inquired, automatically feeling in my pocket.

She beamed upon me like a high priestess initiating some favorite novice into a rite.

"Buttercup Day," she said winningly.

A man of greater strength of mind would no doubt have asked what Buttercup Day was, but I have a spine of wax. I produced the first decent-sized coin on which my fumbling fingers rested and slipped it into her money box. She thanked me with a good deal of fervor and pinned one of the yellow objects in my buttonhole.

The incident brought home to P.G. the question of mortality, but he concluded philosophically: 'Oh well, it's all in a lifetime!'

In the same letter, he talks of the death of his English publisher.

> Herbert Jenkins' death was a great shock to me. I was awfully fond of him, but I always had an idea he could not last very long. He simply worked himself to death. He was very fragile with a terrific driving mind and no physique at all, one of those fellows who look transparent and are always tired. One used to wonder how long he could possibly carry on. He shirked his meals and exercise and concentrated entirely on work. You can't do it.

P.G. stayed on with the firm, though, who had already published nine of his works.

The Bolton-Wodehouse-Berlin show *Sitting Pretty* had now opened, but was only a moderate success. P.G., of course, was hard at work on a new novel, but this time in very different surroundings. Ethel had decided that as her husband was now a successful author, he ought to live like one, and she therefore secured a large and luxurious house in Grosvenor Square. Ethel loved it, and P.G. was glad she loved it. He didn't love it; the set-up was too formal to allow him the freedom to work, for it is often forgotten that in between parties and signing title-pages, even the most famous authors have actually to write books. As he said to Townend: 'We have damned dinners and lunches that just eat up the time. I find that having a lunch hanging over me kills my morning's work, and dinner isn't much better. I'm at the stage now, if I drop my characters, they go cold.'

The work didn't stop, though, and *Sam the Sudden, Carry On, Jeeves* and *The Heart of a Goof* were published in fairly quick succession. Then P.G. was on the move again. In 1926, a friend of Ethel, Charles le Strange, invited them both to spend the summer at his home, Hunstanton Hall in Norfolk. Plum felt in need of a little rural peace, and having been assured that the house was utterly huge, and hence peaceful, he set off. As it turned out, he loved the house, and found all the peace he needed. He wrote in a boat on the moat. With his typewriter, naturally. In a letter to Townend, he fills in a bit of colour: 'There is a duck close by which utters occasional quacks that sound like a man with an unpleasant voice saying nasty things in an undertone.'

By the end of the year, P.G. was back in New York working with Guy Bolton and George Gershwin. The musical was *Oh! Kay!*, and starred Gertrude Lawrence. A hit! A hit! – and possibly one of their greatest; it seemed to be the 'Oh!' that did it. As was the way with this sort of thing, really stinging success prompted all sorts of commissions from every quarter, three of which were accepted. Words and music flooded out, and almost a year elapsed before the Wodehouses returned to England.

Whereupon Ethel surpassed herself.

The opening page of a 1925 Saturday Evening Post *contribution.*

Plum being quite
convincing in
Hunstanton Hall
in 1928,
wearing plus-fours
at the very least.

There was no doubt at all that Plum's coffers were by now positively bulging with the green stuff, and so it was surely the moment, Ethel judged, to slightly ease the strain on the hinges. Rich and famous authors, she thought, ought to be seen to be rich and famous authors. Consequently, at a rent of over £100 a week (the year is 1927) she secured an extremely lavish house just off Park Lane, Mayfair. Having bought a Rolls-Royce, and hired a chauffeur to drive the thing, she also gathered up a secretary or two, a cook, a kitchen maid, a footman, two housemaids, a few other below-stairs odds and ends and, of course, a butler. And then she redecorated the whole place.

Now, P.G. didn't mind any of this; in fact, it pleased him to see her so happy. Anyway, he was writing at the time. Ethel furnished a proper 'author's study' for him as well: panelled walls, tasteful antiques, even a complete library of leather-bound things, books. He thanked her enthusiastically, though never actually got around to going into the room. He typed on a kitchen table in his bedroom. The typewriter, incidentally, was still the old Monarch which he had bought on that very early American trip.

All this was tolerable, however. P.G. even felt quite indulgent. What he truly could not get down, though, was the inevitable consequence of such a wheeze – i.e. the import of gangs of people to view the whole thing, who would be duly envious, humbled, nosy or rude. In a word, entertaining. Quite the social lioness, Ethel held endless cocktail parties at the cocktail hour, as well as not a few fully-fledged dinner parties. If pushed, P.G. would put in an appearance at one or two of these but, more likely, would be found either in his bedroom, writing, or else in Hyde Park, very probably thinking about writing. It was not that he was a recluse exactly, or that he hated people. It was just that these were usually not his sort of people. He also was averse to the implication that he might be seen to be displaying his wealth or success. All he really wanted people to see of him was in his books. He was, as you can gather, a man of simple tastes; fine food did not interest him, and nor did the elaborate cocktails of the time. Wooster he wasn't. He smoked about an ounce of tobacco a day in one of his many pipes – in his later years taking to filling them with broken cigars – and had maybe a couple of dry Martinis. One of his main objections to the ritual of eating, of course, was the time it took, precious time, of which he now spent a fair deal in Hyde Park, walking the dog. His disinterest in the opulence of the new house is implicit in the opening line of a letter to Townend, written from that address: 'We have got a new Peke, Susan, three months old.' That was the main excitement of the moment, and the bond grew. Susan was soon the utterly favourite dog, and more or less Plum's best friend, in that she accompanied him more often and to more places than any other living soul. In P.G.'s view, the new hound was the cat's whiskers, and so it was a matter of course that she should trot along with the

The 1927 Broadway production of Her Cardboard Lover, *adapted by Wodehouse.*

Wodehouses to Hunstanton Hall, which in 1927 they had rented for the summer.

And then Ziegfeld called. When Ziegfeld called, people had a habit of hearing, and so Plum was soon back in America, scribbling away lyrics with Ira Gershwin for brother George's music, and George Grossmith's book. *The Three Musketeers* was the result, and this was rapidly followed by P.G.'s own play, *Good Morning, Bill*. That year also saw the first night of *Showboat*, and although this really had nothing to do with P.G., Kern had included a song that they had written together many years before, and shelved. The song was called 'Bill' and it became Plum's most famous lyric.

The next year he was back in London, and he wrote to Townend from his Park Lane palace in a relatively relaxed mood. He was, after all, working on only two novels at the time.

> Can you get anything to read these days? I was in *The Times* Library yesterday and came out empty-handed. There wasn't a thing I wanted. To fill in the time before Edgar Wallace writes another one, I am re-reading Dunsany.

RIGHT: *Four first editions :* Meet Mr. Mulliner *(1927)*, Summer Lightning *(1929)*, Very Good, Jeeves *(1930), and* Hot Water *(1932)*.

BELOW: *Plum's celebrated lyric, the song 'Bill', set to Jerome Kern's music and made famous by* Showboat.

SONG, "BILL." MARIE BURKE.

I used to dream that I'd discover
The perfect lover some day.
I knew I'd recognize him if ever
He came around my way.

I always used to fancy then
He'd be one of the God-like kind of men,
With a giant brain and a noble head.

Jake (**Michael Cole**)

But along came Bill, who's not the type at all.

MEET Mr. MULLINER
P.G. WODEHOUSE

FOR
SUMMARY
OF THIS STORY
SEE
BACK OF
WRAPPER

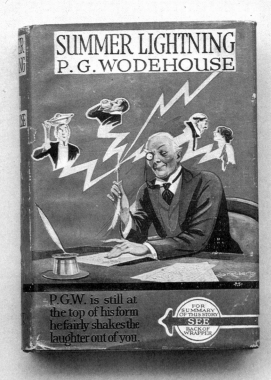

SUMMER LIGHTNING
P.G. WODEHOUSE

P.G.W. is still at
the top of his form
he fairly shakes the
laughter out of you.

FOR
SUMMARY
OF THIS STORY
SEE
BACK OF
WRAPPER

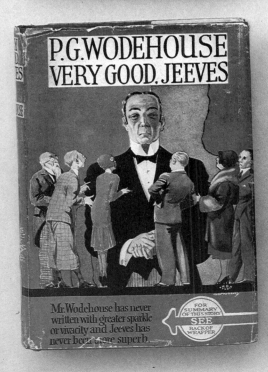

P.G. WODEHOUSE
VERY GOOD. JEEVES

Mr. Wodehouse has never
written with greater sparkle
or vivacity and Jeeves has
never been more superb.

FOR
SUMMARY
OF THIS STORY
SEE
BACK OF
WRAPPER

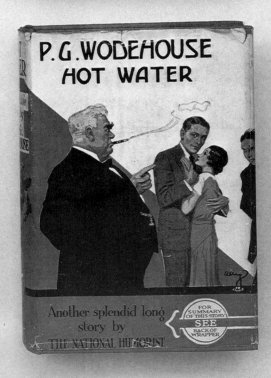

P.G. WODEHOUSE
HOT WATER

Another splendid long
story by
THE NATIONAL HUMORIST

FOR
SUMMARY
OF THIS STORY
SEE
BACK OF
WRAPPER

Knowing Wallace, he probably didn't have long to wait. Talking still of Wallace, P.G. tells Townend that he 'now has a Rolls-Royce and also a separate car for each of the five members of his family. Also a day butler and a night butler, so that you can never go into his house and not find buttling going on. That's the way to live!'

Not that he believed it, of course, for he was himself living in much the same way, and finding it resistible. He was a great fan of Edgar Wallace, though, and a few years earlier had dedicated *Sam the Sudden* to him, Wallace reciprocating with his *The Gaunt Stranger*. Later on, P.G. came to greatly admire and enjoy Agatha Christie. Intrigue intrigued, and thrillers rather thrilled him.

That summer he was writing again to Townend, this time from Rogate Lodge, Sussex, which he had rented for the season. There were people all over the place, including Denis Mackail and Michael Arlen. As P.G. writes: 'We have been getting quite social lately. Guests in every nook and cranny. John Galsworthy came to lunch yesterday – he has a house near here – and we also had Leslie Howard.' Only one who knew Plum less well than Townend would have mistaken the opening lines for enthusiasm. P.G. still didn't like dinners, or dressing for them, and he still tended to buzz off at will. But Ethel, anyway, was happy about the whole thing. As for Plum, as he says in a later letter: 'I have spent the summer writing and rewriting *Summer Lightning*, and must have done – all told – about 100,000 words.' Not that he found this in the least daunting, or even adequate, for in the same letter he asks:

> Have you any short story plots you want to dispose of? I need a Lord Emsworth plot and also a Ukridge. I am planning a vast campaign. I want to write six short stories simultaneously. I have three plots to begin with, and I want three more. Don't you feel, when writing a story, that if only it were some other story you could write it on your head? I do. I'm sure it's the best way to have two or three going at the same time, so that when you get sick of the characters of one, you can switch to another.

P.G. devoted the rest of the year to the stage. He was collaborating with Ian Hay now, and working for Ziegfeld both in New York and at Hunstanton Hall. And all the time, P.G. was still learning his craft. In a couple of letters to Townend at this time, he wrote:

> The longer I write, the more I realise the necessity for telling a story as far as possible in *scenes*, especially at the start . . . . What a sweat a novel is till you are sure of your characters. And what a vital thing it is to have plenty of things for a major character to *do*. That is the test. If they aren't in situations, characters can't be major characters, not even if you have the rest of the troupe talk their heads off about them.

The theatrical evidence is even stronger here, and not only in the use of the word 'troupe'. Sam Goldwyn must have noticed P.G.'s appreciation of the importance of 'scenes' in writing, for he now expressed interest in P.G. as a potential writer for the Silver Screen. In Hollywood, where else?

It was Ethel who went over to the States to negotiate Plum's contract. She eventually closed on a deal with MGM for a six-month contract, with an option for a further six months at a salary of $2000. Per week. She was wise to close on such a deal; all that money, and the Hollywood lights to boot.

The Yuletide season was spent with the le Stranges, as their guests, but, as P.G. wrote to Townend: 'I'm glad Christmas is over. I came in for the New Year festivities at Hunstanton, and had to wear a white waistcoat every night.'

P.G. Wodehouse, beau.

Plum in 1928 – probably at Hunstanton Hall – with Ian Hay
(to say nothing of the dogs).

CHAPTER EIGHT

AMERICA, I LIKE YOU

ollywood in 1930 was quite a place. Dreams were made here, and P.G. trotted off to write a few. Leonora accompanied him and Ethel was to follow later, possibly feeling that a slow run-up was required to this ultimate Mecca of society. P.G. quite liked the place and wrote to Townend in appreciation of the house he was staying in. It belonged to Norma Shearer, and had a swimming pool and everything else one might expect. Plum kept his feet on the ground, though. His summing-up of the West's most glittering acres went as follows:

Odd place this. Miles and miles of one-story *(sic)* bungalows, mostly Spanish, each with a little lawn in front and a pocket-handkerchief garden at the back, all jammed together in rows. Beverley Hills, where I am, is the rather aristocratic sector. Very pretty. Our house has a garden the size of the garden of any small house in Dulwich, and we pay two hundred quid a month for it.

Howsomever, if P.G. was underwhelmed by the glamour, he did find the place conducive to work, for in less than a month he had produced 'three short stories, an act of a play, and all the dialogue for a picture.' At times, of course, one feels that Plum would have found a coal cellar prone to rising damp conducive to work, but nonetheless, Hollywood seemed to please him – possibly because he didn't see anyone much, didn't go anywhere much, and usually dined *à deux* with Leonora.

ABOVE: *Mr and Mrs Sam Goldwyn around 1930, about to embark on a cruise. The original caption reads 'Mr. Goldwyn is a noted motion picture man'. Yes.*

ABOVE: *Wodehouse, pictured in 1930, arriving at Los Angeles to embark upon his Hollywood stint, accompanied by his step-daughter Leonora.*

LEFT: *A typical Los Angeles boulevard in 1930.*

BELOW: *Is it a bird? Is it a plane? No, it's a gorgeously Art Deco MGM publicity car, fuelled by coloured balloons.*

And then Ethel came, and things changed rather. For Ethel, this was the big one. The Wodehouses were asked to all the fashionable and lavish parties, and, in the nicest possible way, they threw loads of them back. The champagne bubbled, and so did Ethel, for simply *everyone*, don't you know, was there. For a time, life for P.G. was one long voguish bunfight, and he rarely encountered anyone who could or would exchange a word about writing. Or Pekes. Or cricket. Only one woman at a party praised his books – said she had read every one; it only later transpired that she was under the impression that she had been talking to Edgar Wallace.

Plum still wrote, though, but almost totally the sort of stuff he would have written anywhere: stories, a novel, play ideas. The MGM studio didn't seem to have too much for him to do, so he picked up the $2000 a week, and Ethel threw parties. By the end of the six months, Hollywood lost any fascination it might once have had. P.G. had had enough of doing nothing (nothing, that is, for MGM) and he wanted to get back to England. MGM, however, seemed quite eager for him to do nothing for a little longer, for they took up the further six-month option clause in the contract. Ah well, at least the weather was nice.

Plum made a few friends in the meantime. Gerard Fairlie – who was in Hollywood to write the Bulldog Drummond films – was staying with him, and Maureen O'Sullivan dropped in quite a lot. She too was a Peke enthusiast, though Winks – Plum's Peke of the Month, and son of Susan – did not take over-kindly to the O'Sullivan pooch. Not a great mixer, Winks.

Life trundled along, and then Wodehouse gave an interview to *The Los Angeles Times* concerning his stay with MGM. It was not the last time that P.G. would be castigated for merely saying what he thought; there was no guile in Wodehouse, you see. The interview when printed caused an almighty stir, and this is why:

> They paid me $2000 a week – $104,000 – and I cannot see what they engaged me for. They were extremely nice to me, but I feel as if I have cheated them. You see, I understood I was engaged to write stories for the screen . . . Twice during the year they brought completed scenarios of other people's stories to me and asked me to do some dialogue. Fifteen or sixteen people had tinkered with these stories. The dialogue was really quite adequate. All I did was to touch it up here and there. Then they set me to work on a story called *Rosalie* which was to have some musical numbers. It was a pleasant little thing, and I put in three months on it. When it was finished, they thanked me politely and remarked that as musicals didn't seem to be going so well they guessed they would not use it. That about sums up what I was called upon to do for my $104,000. Isn't it amazing? . . . It's so unbelievable, isn't it?

Plum in 1930, at the age of forty-nine.

A scene from the 1935 London production of Anything Goes — *a Wodehouse/Bolton/ Porter collaboration.*

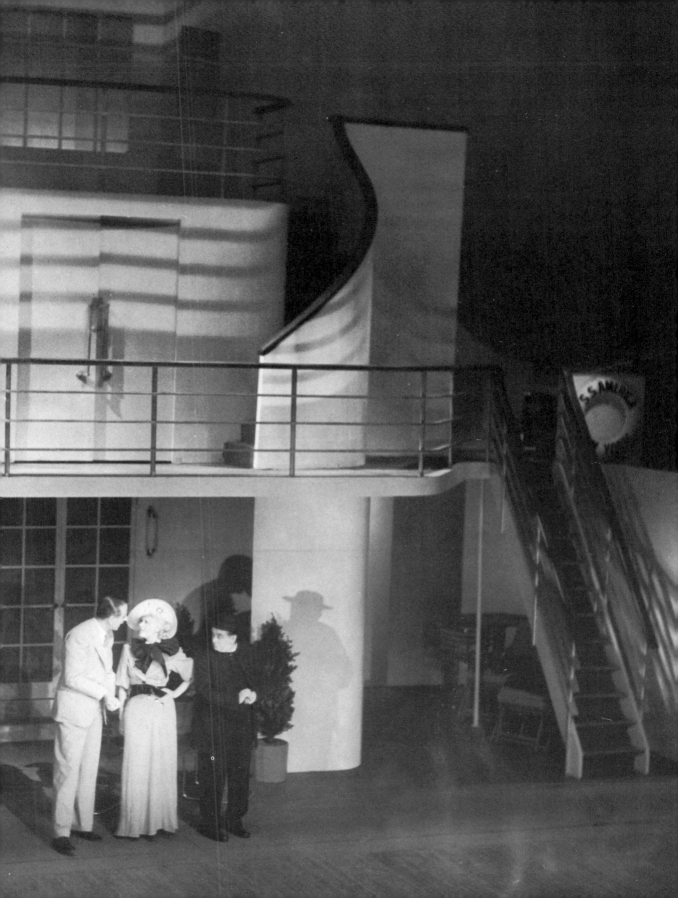

When this little lot hit the newstands, Hollywood was shaken. Many writers who had been receiving a similar salary in return for comparable effort were outraged. More importantly, though, the banks were not happy, and when the banks were not happy Hollywood ceased to smile. Stories of extravagance, waste and opulence were all very well for the fan magazines – indeed, they were seen to be necessary – but such clear evidence from a famous and level-headed English writer was not so good at all. The banks clamped down, and Wodehouse was not a popular man. Although he had merely said what was true, the combination of fame, innocence and honesty did tend to lead to problems.

Anyway, P.G.'s contract had already expired, and to no-one's surprise, the men in suits at MGM did not seem to be falling over themselves to renew it. The year had by no means been a write-off, though, for now Plum had two novels almost ready for publication. He pushed off back to England, and the round of writing and reading was resumed. On his reading, the following snippets from letters to Townend give some insight into his current tastes: 'I am at last reading *The Good Companions*. I love it. That's the sort of book I would like to write.' 'I bought Aldous Huxley's *Brave World* thing, but simply can't read it. What a bore these stories of the future are. The whole point of Huxley is that he can write better about modern life than anybody else, so of course he goes and writes about the future, blast him.'

Back in England, P.G. launched into his first Jeeves novel, *Thank you, Jeeves*, though he managed to find time for a holiday on the French Riviera, spending much of it with E. Phillips Oppenheim, with whom P.G. had quite often played golf, and had quite often lost. In a letter to Bill Townend from France, P.G. tells of the life literary on the Riviera:

> H.G. Wells lives not far from here, and I have been seeing him occasionally. He lunched here yesterday. I knew him slightly in London, at the time when he had some complicated row with a man who had worked for him on his *Outline of History*. He asked a bunch of authors to dinner to hear his side of the thing. Why he included me, I don't know. Arnold Bennett was there, and we walked home together. He was pleasant but patronizing.
>
> I like Wells. An odd bird, though. The first time I met him, we had barely finished the initial pip-pippings when he said, apropos of nothing, 'My father was a professional cricketer.' If there's a good answer to that, you tell me. I thought of saying 'Mine had a white moustache,' but finally settled for 'Oh, ah', and we went on to speak of other things.

In point of fact, Wodehouse's father had died just before the Hollywood trip, at the age of eighty-three. There had not been a lot of contact between the two of recent years, though naturally P.G. was affected. Some really splendid family news arrived for Plum now, though, for it appeared that Leonora had got herself engaged to a young man named Peter Cazalet. Ethel and P.G. returned to London that

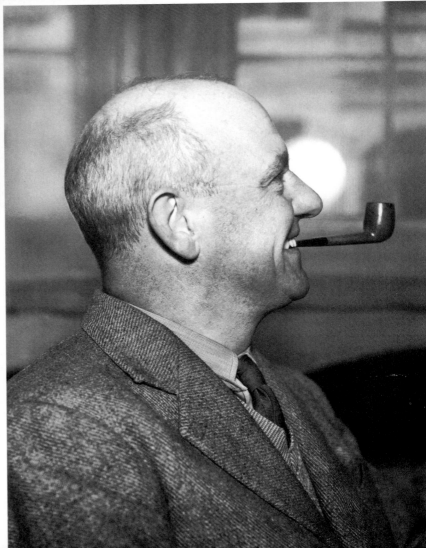

LEFT: *H.G. Wells leaving Waterloo in 1931, bound for the U.S.A.*

BELOW: *P.G. and pipe, in 1933.*

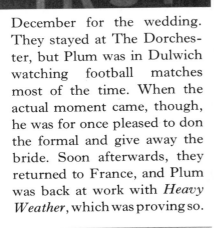

December for the wedding. They stayed at The Dorchester, but Plum was in Dulwich watching football matches most of the time. When the actual moment came, though, he was for once pleased to don the formal and give away the bride. Soon afterwards, they returned to France, and Plum was back at work with *Heavy Weather*, which was proving so.

In a letter to Townend, Wodehouse discusses the problem.

> It's a curious thing about this novel, and probably means that it's going to be good, but I must have written at least 200,000 words so far. For a long time I couldn't get the thing straight. I kept getting dissatisfied with the first 30,000 words and starting again. Today I reached page 254 and have a very detailed scenario of the rest, and all up to page 254 now looks all right. It really reads as if I had written it straight off without a pause.

As does all his work.

While he plugged on with *Heavy Weather*, Jenkins published *Mulliner Nights*, and *Thank you, Jeeves* had been sold to *Cosmopolitan* for $50,000 – Plum's record fee to date. *Heavy Weather*, of course, came out brilliantly and was snapped up by *The Saturday Evening Post*. Plum was back in Mayfair now, and already at work on the second Jeeves novel.

March of 1934 was fairly memorable for Plum, for at the age of fifty-two, he became an almost-grandfather. Leonora had given birth to a little girl named Sharon, with whom Plum was much taken, describing her affectionately as looking like 'an old Chinese gangster'. He must have needed this bit of bucking-up about now, for a couple of weeks prior to the joyous, he was writing to Townend of:

> The foulest week of my career. . . it included two visits to the dentist, a cold in the head, the opening of Crockford's Club (one of these ghastly functions where you're invited for ten o'clock and don't have any dinner because you think supper will be served the moment you arrive and then don't get any supper), an American interviewer who caught me just as the cold was at its worst, and a snack luncheon to celebrate the publication of a young author's new book. And finally, the shifting of our fifteen trunks, twenty suitcases and two Pekes . . .
>
> I must say that luncheon was the limit. It seemed to take one into a new and dreadful world. Can you imagine giving a lunch to celebrate the publication of a book? With other authors, mostly fairies, twittering all over the place, screaming 'Oh Lionel!' and photographs of you holding the book, etc. Gosh! Dumas was the boy. When he had finished a novel he kept on sitting and started another. No snack luncheons for him.

Despite the humour here, this is quite a heated outburst, for Plum. That 'Gosh!' comes straight from the heart, and he meant it to sting.

The Luck of the Bodkins was P.G.'s next venture, and again the going seemed rather tough. He wrote from Paris to Townend: 'I find that the longer I go on writing, the harder it becomes to get a story right without going over and over it. I

Four first editions : Heavy Weather *(1933),* Right Ho, Jeeves *(1934),* Blandings Castle *(1935), and* The Luck of the Bodkins *(1935).*

P. G. WODEHOUSE
HEAVY WEATHER

"Mr. Wodehouse (bless
him!) is never dull
he is superb" PUNCH

FOR
SUMMARY
OF THIS STORY
SEE
BACK OF
WRAPPER

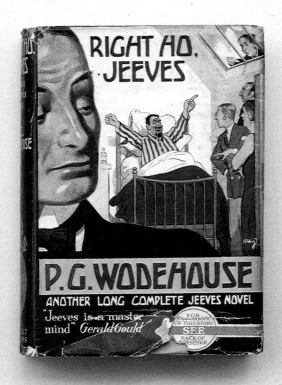

RIGHT HO,
JEEVES

P. G. WODEHOUSE
ANOTHER LONG COMPLETE JEEVES NOVEL
"Jeeves is a master
mind" Gerald Gould

FOR
SUMMARY
OF THIS STORY
SEE
BACK OF
WRAPPER

P. G. WODEHOUSE
BLANDINGS CASTLE

FOR
SUMMARY
OF THIS STORY
SEE
BACK OF
WRAPPER

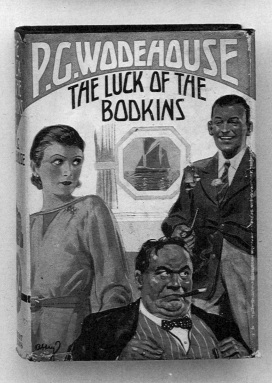

P. G. WODEHOUSE
THE LUCK OF THE
BODKINS

have just reached page 180 and I suppose I must have done quite 400 pages'. Six months later he wrote:

> Meanwhile *The Luck of the Bodkins* was coming out with great difficulty. Have you had the experience of getting out what looks like a perfect scenario and then finding that it won't write and has to be completely changed? . . . Usually when I get to the last 50 pages of a story it begins to write itself. But this time everything went wrong and I had to grope my way through it all at the rate of 2 pages a day. I began to get superstitious about it and felt that if I could ever get it finished my luck would be in.

It seems as if Plum's superstitions were not unfounded, for although he did finish, a couple of months later he was delivering unto Townend the following bombshell. 'Hell's foundations quivering briskly just now. *The Saturday Evening Post* have rejected *The Luck of the Bodkins* – my first rejection in America in 21 years.'

This at least bears out *The Post's* claim to judge the work and not the name. How did P.G. feel about it? Was he bitter? Did he believe *The Post* to be peopled by unseeing baboons? No. The letter continues:

> I have re-read the book as critically as if it were someone else's – all right someone's else, if you prefer it – and see now what's wrong. Gosh, isn't it awful the mistakes one can make and not see till too late? It's 25,000 words too long.
>
> Do you know, I believe over-longness is the worst fault in writing. I had such a good farcical plot in this one that I got all hopped up and felt that it wasn't possible to give 'em too much of this superb stuff, so every scene I wrote was elaborated till it lost its grip. To give you some idea, I now reach on page 45 a situation which in the original I got to on page 100! That's 15,000 words out for a start. I expect to cut 30,000.

The novel was sold a month later to *The Red Book*, for $25,000 'as against the $40,000 *The Post* would have paid me, but what of it? "Ooh-la-la!" as we say over here.'

'Over here' was France, as one might have gathered, and Le Touquet in particular. Plum had recently bought a house here called Low Wood, and was collaborating with Guy Bolton on a new musical, *Anything Goes*. Or at least he should have been, but as he explains in a letter, 'I'm having a devil of a time. . . I can't get hold of Guy, or the composer Cole Porter. What has become of Cole, Heaven knows. Last heard of at Heidelberg.'

Plum loved the house, though. It was small, and cosy, and in the middle of nowhere, the fetching of the morning papers necessitating a four-mile walk with the dogs. For more or less the same reasons, however, Ethel didn't like it at all. *C'est la vie*, as they say over there. In an attempt to jazz up the place, she brought home a

The song-writer and composer Cole Porter in 1933, at the age of forty.

new Peke called Wonder, whereupon the resident duo, Winks and Boo, sulked for several weeks. Plum was pleased, though. In his view, there could be no such thing as a Peke too many.

The stories continued to flow, and another play was in progress, but Plum was never really happy unless something major was on the go. As he wrote to Townend, though: 'I can't get an idea for a novel. Maddening.' Apart from the work in hand, however, there was always something to do. 'Just had a testing job – reading the page proofs of the Mulliner Omnibus book. 864 pages! It humbled me a good deal, as the stuff didn't seem good. Still, I suppose nothing would, if you read 864 pages of it straight off.'

The place where people leave their mark –
Grauman's Chinese Theatre restaurant, Hollywood.

Around this time he spent a short while with his brother Armine, visiting their mother in Bexhill. But soon he was back in London for the opening of *Anything Goes*. It proved a great success, but was to be the last Bolton-Wodehouse collaboration. Plum had always dearly loved his closest friends, and it was in December of 1935 that he wrote to Townend announcing the death of one of the best:

Isn't it perfectly rotten – my old typewriter on which I have been working since 1911, has gone phut. I had it patched up in Boulogne, but now the shift-key won't work, so I have had to discard it. I am writing this on a machine which has been knocking around for a year or so, while Ethel buys me a new one in London. I think she is getting a Royal. I believe that's what you use, isn't it?

Do you know if there is any way of having my old machine entirely rebuilt? Expense no object. My trouble is that this is a Monarch, and there is no Monarch firm now. Perhaps if I buy a Royal, the Royal people would fix it up.

Don't you find that after you've used a typewriter for a long time, you can't get used to the touch of any other?

It was only the demise of the noble Monarch that was troubling him at the moment, and certainly not the Le Touquet solitude. He goes on:

I have been alone here with the dogs for exactly two weeks tomorrow. It's extraordinary how well one gets along – once one has fallen into a routine. I find the great thing is having something good to read after dinner. The rest of the day takes care of itself.

And this is precisely how this very rich and internationally famous author saw life. Fame and money quite genuinely meant nothing. He only quoted the enormous fees he received in his letters to Townend because he saw them as measures of the quality of his writing; he never really saw it in terms of cash. Indeed, when he did go out shopping, he quite often forgot to bring any money with him – he simply did not think in those terms. As to fame, he was always gratified by some accolade or award which pertained to his work (such as the Mark Twain medal for his 'outstanding and lasting contribution to the happiness of the world' which he received that year) but he could never understand why people should wish to meet him, or invite him to functions. And nor could he understand why people seemed eager to know about him or his life. As he said, 'Just writing one book after another, that's my life.'

Nonetheless, he was very much in demand. Critics who had for years been praising the funniness of his books, began to talk now of the writing, the brilliance of the creator. The word 'genius' had started to creep in, but as yet it was still qualified, as in 'Wodehouse's genius for fun' or 'Wodehouse's special genius lies in . . . ' There was no doubt about it: some years ago P.G. had arrived; it was now clear that he was here to stay. Even Hollywood had forgotten its grievance. The previous year he had written to Townend: 'I had an offer from Paramount the other day to go to Holly-

wood, and had to refuse. But rather gratifying after the way Hollywood took a solemn vow three years ago never to mention my name again. Quite the olive branch!'

Another of which was now extended, this time by his old chums, MGM. Who else to negotiate the contract but Ethel? She managed $2,500 a week this time, and they were off. By now, P.G. was an older man and a wiser man – a step-grandfather for the second time, no less – and he felt that in exchange for all that lettuce, and in view of the notorious *Los Angeles Times* interview, he would be called on to actually write something. He went along to see.

The problem of being unable to find a plot for a novel had finally been solved, and *Laughing Gas* was sent up, though admittedly the plot was adapted from an earlier short story. At this stage, too, P.G. seems conscious of passing time. He wrote to Townend:

RIGHT: *Arthur Treacher in the film role of Jeeves, here caught in the act of being pained by the young master's taste.*

LEFT: *P.G., Ethel and a brace of Pekes aboard the S.S. Normandie in 1936 – arriving in America for a second crack at Hollywood.*

Doesn't Kipling's death give you a sort of stunned feeling? He seems to leave such a gap. I didn't feel the same about Doyle or Bennett or Galsworthy.

I suppose it is because he is so associated with one's boyhood. It has made me feel older all of a sudden.

Older, but still able to adapt, even if a little grudgingly.

I am writing this on my new Royal. I have got quite used to it now, but I still can't feel as easy as I did on the old Monarch – which, I hope, some expert will be able to repair. I don't like these metal things which stick up and hold the paper down, so that you can't get a clear view of what you're writing.

They were soon in the States, and by now Ethel had thoroughly got the hang of this Hollywood thing. The second that she had assured herself that Mr Gayelord Hauser's house in Beverley Hills had the requisite number of staircases and pools, she rented it for $1000 a month. Without pausing for breath she hired a gaggle of flunkeys, including a Japanese butler, which made a change. This done, there seemed nothing to prevent the throwing of parties, and so she got on with the job.

Plum in Beverley Hills in 1936. The young thing is a former actress,
'Mrs. Catherine Dale Owen Davis Metzgar, wife of Homer P. Metzgar of N.Y.'. Who else?

Her parties were always a huge success and everyone had a marvellous time; better than this, though, the parties were *talked* about. Ethel has since admitted that such hoolies were not at all difficult to mount, providing one was earning at least $2500 a week. The thing to do, apparently, was to buy more or less one of every animal one could think of, roast each and float the whole on a reservoir of Bollinger. The rest seemed to take care of itself. Such a formula might be found handy.

P.G., meanwhile, was keen to see in what ways Hollywood had changed in the interim. Action started pretty soon. Someone hit him with the script of *Rosalie*, which had been given to him and taken away again four years earlier. A couple of months later, they whipped it back. But Plum knew the road by now, and he set to on a novel. Another film was on the way, though. As he wrote to Townend:

> Haven't seen many celebrities yet. We don't see much of anybody except our beloved Maureen O'Sullivan' – she of the Pekes – 'and her husband John Farrow. I met Clark Gable the other day. Also Fred Astaire. I think Fred is going to do a picture of my *A Damsel in Distress*, with music by George Gershwin. I shall know more about this later.

Everything stopped, though, when P.G. heard of the death of his brother Armine. This shook him deeply, and he was distressed too by the fact that for some reason the news had taken a month to reach him. As he was committed with MGM, though, he felt totally and maddeningly helpless, and so Ethel returned to England alone to stay with Armine's widow.

But Plum eventually rallied round and plunged into a new novel, *Summer Moonshine*. This he finished just as his MGM contract expired; as before, they had been paying him to write novels. *The Saturday Evening Post* chipped in too, with their customary and welcome $40,000. MGM failed to take up the six-month option this time, though, but P.G. hung around for a while. However, Hollywood had palled. He gave Townend a typical snippet of local news:

> Woman out here has just got a divorce. Stated that her husband had not worked for months and was a pretty low-down character altogether. 'He was always going to dances' she said, 'and when he wanted to go to one the other night, he took the only pair of silk stockings I had and cut the tops off so that he could wear them as socks.'

Wodehouse and Townend were now, in P.G.'s phrase, 'old buffers of 55', and the correspondence was in full swing. Plum wasn't too delighted with life, though, as may be seen from these comments in letters over a six-month period.

> I am getting very fed up with life here. . . I must say I would like to be nearer home. This place seems very far away sometimes. . . I wish we had taken this house for six months instead of a year . . . I'm not enjoying life much just now. I I don't like doing pictures.

And finally, the crunch.

> We have got a big party on tomorrow night – seventy people coming.

He bucked up, though, when R-K-O finally commissioned him to do his own *A Damsel in Distress*. This seemed sure-fire. It was to star Fred Astaire, George Burns and Gracie Allen. And the music was by Gershwin. He enjoyed this work immensely, but then regretted immediately taking on another film, about which he soon discovered that he liked absolutely nothing. This prompted him to write: 'As a rule pictures are a bore.'

P.G. had now had enough. He beetled back to Le Touquet and charged into *The Code of the Woosters*, but although it turned out to be one of his most brilliant, he didn't find the going easy. By January 1938, he was writing to Townend:

> I am finding finishing *The Code of the Woosters* a ghastly sweat. I don't seem to have the drive and command of words I used to. Towards the end of *Thank you, Jeeves*, at La Frèyere, I wrote 26 pages one day. Now I find myself quarrying out the stuff.

He got through it eventually, though, and almost immediately embarked on *Uncle Fred in the Springtime*, which proved to be another headache. 'I have been sweating like blazes getting a new novel started,' he wrote, but also mentioned that great rejoicing had recently been the scene in the Wodehouse home, for Winky the Peke was ten years old. A cake was provided, naturally, with 'Happy Birthday' on it. In white sugar. Sadly, though, within six months of this joyous event, poor old Winks had handed in his dinner pail. Another blow came in the shape of *The Saturday Evening Post*'s suggestion that he cut and alter *Uncle Fred in the Springtime*. Radically. He agreed to do this, but found that for the job to be done properly a complete re-write was necessary. So he re-wrote.

The year was now 1939, and critical acclaim for Plum was growing all the time. He was at the very peak of his powers and of his popularity. He was thus extremely honoured when on the 21st of June Oxford University bestowed upon him the Doctorate of Letters, and he had no hesitation in travelling from Le Touquet to receive the degree. He was a very popular and deserving choice. As *The Times* leader put it the following morning:

> There is no question that in making Mr P.G. Wodehouse a doctor of letters the University has done the right and popular thing. Everyone knows at least some of his many works and has felt all the better for the gaiety of his wit and the freshness of his style. Style goes a long way in Oxford; indeed the purity of Mr Wodehouse's

A still from the 1936 MGM film Piccadilly Jim, *starring Robert Montgomery, with the gentleman's gentleman being played by Eric Blore.*

ABOVE: *The inimitable Fred Astaire in the film* A Damsel in Distress.
He has just buckled his swash, and is ready to foil again.

RIGHT: *The R-K-O 1937 film* A Damsel in Distress.
Fred Astaire, Gracie Allen and George Burns distort the truth.

style was singled out for particular praise in the Public Orator's happy Horatian summing up of Mr Wodehouse's qualities and achievements.

There is no doubt that P.G. felt proud as he followed the procession through the Oxford streets. Neither is there any denying that as the ceremony had called for the donning of wing collar and gown, to say nothing of the mortarboard, he also felt something of a silly ass. But then he had learnt that one can rarely do anything pleasant without first assuming some frightful costume or other, which in his view took the edge off the whole thing.

Thus far into 1939, if there was any feeling of foreboding from abroad, Wodehouse was aware of none of it. Politics, like religion, were of no interest to him, this fact possibly going some way to explaining his general contentment with things. However, famous people could not afford to be unaware, as he was quite soon to discover. P.G. was back in Le Touquet when, on the 3rd of September, Britain declared war on Germany.

Feelings about the Nazi countries of course ran high in Britain, but Wodehouse was not really aware of this either. He appreciated that Germany was the enemy, of course, and that – as far as he could see – was surely that.

But feelings change, and things are very rapidly viewed differently. The Mark Twain medal, you will remember, was given to P.G. in 1936 in recognition of his 'outstanding and lasting contribution to the happiness of the world'. Previous recipients included Kipling, Roosevelt, Marconi, and also Benito Mussolini. Times, then, had changed, but Plum was never very good at keeping up. He was never that interested in keeping up.

P.G. and Sir H.J.C. Grierson, each having just received a Doctorate of Letters from Oxford University, in 1939.

CHAPTER NINE

SUMMER LIGHTNING

I'm not absolutely certain of my facts, but I rather fancy it's Shakespeare – or, if not, it's some equally brainy bird – who says that it's always just when a fellow is feeling particularly braced with things in general that Fate sneaks up behind him with the bit of lead piping. And what I'm driving at is that the man is perfectly right.

CARRY ON, JEEVES

In Le Touquet, as in England, nothing much happened immediately following the declaration of war. Life jogged along much as usual for a while, and though it is true that many people resident in France very quickly returned to their own countries, quite as many did not, as there really didn't seem much reason for doing so. The Wodehouses were among those who stayed. Quite early in 1940, however, news of an imminent German invasion eventually reached Le Touquet, but by that time it was too late to do anything about it. A man aware of the feel of things really would have left by now, but Wodehouse wasn't, and consequently hadn't; interestingly, neither had anyone advised him to.

He had a try, though. The last RAF plane to fly out offered him a seat, but there was no room for Ethel, to say nothing of the Pekes, so that was out. They made an attempt to reach the coast by road, but the car broke down, wouldn't you know. The occupation of Le Touquet duly took place in May, and Low Wood was placed 'under surveillance'. Once a day, P.G. had to report to the German authorities, which he did, and this pattern continued for about three months. It was beginning to seem that even a German invasion did little to ruffle one's way of life, for Plum rather enjoyed a good walk. Things turned ugly, though, and rapidly. P.G.'s entire world was about to be stood on its head. By June, the Germans had reached Paris, and the Franco-German armistice was signed. Britain was now the sole enemy of Germany, and British citizens were to be viewed in a fresh light. One morning in July, P.G. made his daily trip to the *Kommandatur*, and was briskly informed that all male aliens were to be interned, immediately. He was escorted back to Low Wood and told to pack a few essentials. They would be leaving straight away.

P.G. reeled. He did not quite believe that this sort of thing happened. Both he and Ethel were extremely shaken. He had very quickly to assemble what he considered to be the necessities of life, and hastily decided upon tobacco, pipes, paper, pens, a razor, tea, a Tennyson and a Shakespeare. To this he added a few clothes. Within hours, P.G. was on a bus with a dozen other internees, on their way to Loos prison, seventy-five miles from Le Touquet.

The internees were registered upon arrival, the crime of most of them being that they were English. P.G. was put into a cell with two others. The cell was originally intended for one man only, and only one bed was provided. As P.G. was not the oldest of the three men, he had to do without. It was an extremely small room, and very much a cell in every way – stone floor, tiny barred window, and an iron door replete with flapped peephole. Within the cell, in addition to the bed, there was a tap, a latrine, and a chair chained to the wall, though where a prisoner might have been disposed to take the thing, God knows. P.G. was a week at Loos, twenty-three out of every twenty-four hours being spent in the cell. Three times a day he received a bowl of sort of soup, a piece of bread, and some water. At the end of the week, the prisoners learned that everyone over the age of sixty would be released, and all others were to be moved. P.G. computed with despair that he was not yet fifty-nine, and so soon found himself at the railway station with hundreds of men similarly unfortunate. There they were crushed into cattle trucks so tightly that it was possible only to stand and do nothing else at all. The journey was to last nineteen hours, at the end of which they found themselves in Liege, Belgium. They were met by the S.S.

The S.S. had not yet acquired their vile notoriety at this early stage of the war, and their methods were as yet largely untried. They were to act, then, only as escorts. The internees marched for miles in the Belgian countryside, which, coming immediately after so appalling a train journey, cannot have been welcomed by the men, most of whom were in their fifties. They eventually reached an old barracks, their new prison. More watery soup was doled out. The place was in a quite loathsome condition, and the prisoners did their best to clean it up a bit. It was a fairly squalid place, but better than Loos, in that each man at least had a bed. Indeed, as the soup – occasionally - contained a potato, one was free to be in the open air, and a sort of coffee was served, it seemed comparatively good. They were there only one week, though, and were then once more on the move. Again the men were crammed into cattle trucks; six hours later they arrived in Huy, and the massive and stone prison called The Citadel. It was, however, designed for a quarter the number of men who were now about to occupy it. Not only were there very few beds, but even blankets were scarce. Inmates were allowed to write to their wives, though, and one imagines Ethel's pain on receiving Plum's request for a blanket. She sent him a caseful.

The menu was the usual rather watery soup and soupy water, but less of it. The daily ration was two mugs of coffee, one bowl of soup and a piece of bread. It was

The War years. P.G. with an acquaintance in Berlin in 1942.

not much, but P.G. missed tobacco more than food, for he had not brought a lot with him, and it was now all gone. He smoked his tea until that ran out too.

P.G. spent five weeks at Huy, during which he kept a diary. He sent this to Bill Townend in 1952, together with *The Camp Book* – writings about his later prison experiences at Tost. This book, characteristically, he subtitled *Wodehouse in Wonderland*. In the covering letter to Townend, P.G. states unequivocally: 'It will never be published, but I hope it will amuse you.' From the Huy diary it is very clear what sort of a place it was, and the hardships are recorded, though always with humour. Occasionally, the whole experience sounds like a public school jape, though the seriousness and unpleasantness of the period come home pretty forcibly.

> Our first night was not so bad as I thought it was going to be. At the last moment we were moved to a larger room, and somebody suddenly remembered that there was straw in the cellars, so we went and fetched it – a hundred and ten steps down and ditto up. There was only enough to form a very thin deposit on the floor, and it stank to high heaven. Still, it was straw.

Which, when the mood took him, P.G. would smoke in his pipe. There is no record of how this compared with tea.

> Our buckets contained a sort of sweet hot water with prunes floating in it. I have seldom tasted anything so loathsome, but it was really rather a *tour de force* on the part of our cook, for it is not easy to brew soup for 800 men on a foundation of 28lbs of macaroni. In adding prunes I think he overstressed the bizarre note, but I suppose he had to add something. A less conscientious man might have put in a couple of small Belgians.

A small Belgian vamoosed one day, P.G. describing the atmosphere at Huy as 'rather like Dotheboys Hall after escape of Smike.' In the same entry, he quotes a Scottish inmate who had once resided in a Glaswegian jail, compared with which Huy was truly luxurious. 'Ye had a wooden pillow, and ye didn't need to turn it over, as it was the same on both sides,' he said.

Food, understandably, was in Plum's thoughts.

> Horrible shock today. The bread ration failed and we each got thirty biscuits instead, about the size of those which restaurants used to give you with your order of oysters. Felt like a tiger which has been offered a cheese straw.
>
> Met cook today and congratulated him on yesterday's soup. He was grateful for my kind words, for his professional pride had been wounded by grumblers who criticised the quantity. He said he could have produced more soup by adding water, but that would have weakened it, and he refused to prostitute his art. I said he was quite right and that it was the same in my business. A short story is a short story. Try to pad it out into a novel and you lose the flavour.

Writing, incidentally, had by no means been forgotten. P.G. had to write, and he could do it anywhere. The saving grace of all his prison experiences was that he was never denied the necessary facilities, and he therefore wrote a lot. At the time of this diary entry, he was working on the scenario for *Money in the Bank*.

His attitude to his German jailers is summed up in the following extract. He does not hate them. He sees them as being quite as confused and well-meaning as everyone else.

> The German soldiers themselves are all right. . . There is one particularly genial sergeant, whose only fault is that he has got entirely the wrong angle on these damned parades. He wants us to go through the motions smartly, with lots of snap. 'Come on, boys,' he seems to be saying. 'Get the Carnival spirit. Switch on the charm. Give us the old personality.'
>
> He actually suggested the other day that we should come on parade at the double. When we were convinced that we had really heard what we thought we had heard, we looked at one another with raised eyebrows and asked Enke to explain to this visionary that in order to attend parade we had to climb twenty-seven steep stone steps. It was unreasonable, we felt, to expect us to behave like mountain goats on a diet of biscuits about the size of aspirin tablets and one small mug of thin soup a day.
>
> 'Try to make him understand,' we urged Enke, 'that it is pretty dashed creditable of us getting on parade at all. Tell him he has sized us up all wrong. We are elderly internees, most of us with corns and swollen joints, not Alpine climbers. If we are supposed to be youths who bear mid snow and ice a banner with the strange device "Excelsior", there ought to be St Bernard dogs stationed here and there, dispensing free brandy. Ask him if he expects us to yodel.'
>
> Enke put these points, and the man saw reason. Only once has our iron front been broken down. That was the day before yesterday, when a spruce young lieutenant, a stranger to us, took over and electrified us suddenly shouting 'Achtung!' in a voice like someone calling the cattle home across the Sands of Dee. It startled us so much that we sprang to attention like a Guards regiment.
>
> But we were waiting for him in the evening. He shouted 'Achtung' again, and didn't get a ripple.

The weeks wore on, P.G. observing and recording.

> A strange new big pot arrives, inspects us, goes through the dormitories and disappears. Probably just someone slumming.

All the inmates, though, were now,

> . . . more or less obsessed with the subject of food. Still no bread. We get nothing but biscuits now, thirty per man and only just visible to the naked eye. It seems to

date from the day when we complained to the Kommandant that we were not getting enough bread. He took the statesmanlike course of giving us no bread at all.

Eventually there came the time when all the internees were told they would be moving again. A couple of days before this, P.G. was musing a bit on the apparent German bafflement as to why they were all there in the first place. He wrote in his diary:

> I'm bound to say the whole thing puzzles me a bit, too. Why Germany should think it worth while to round up and corral a bunch of spavined old deadbeats like myself and the rest of us it is beyond me to imagine. Silly horseplay is the way I look at it.
>
> The idea, I suppose, is that if left at large, we would go about selling the plans of forts. But one would have thought that a single glance at me would have been enough to tell them that if somebody handed me a fort on a plate with watercress round it, I wouldn't know what to do with it.
>
> I wouldn't even know what price to charge.

Nonetheless, this dangerous character now found himself huddled with not a few like desperadoes, on a train which rattled along for three days and nights, each man sustaining himself with a loaf of bread and some soup. One imagines hell, though P.G. describes the journey merely as 'a little trying.'

Eventually, they reached Tost, in Upper Silesia, and were installed in the local lunatic asylum. P.G. describes the place in his *Camp Book*. The humour, and the sanity, shine like beacons.

> Tost is no beauty spot. It lies in the heart of sugar-beet country, and if you are going in for growing sugar-beet on a large scale, you have to make up your mind to dispense with wild, romantic scenery. There is a flat dullness about the countryside which has led many a visitor to say, 'If this is Upper Silesia, what must Lower Silesia be like?' And the charm of any lunatic asylum never strikes you immediately. You have to let it grow on you.
>
> I came in time to be very contented in this Upper Silesian loony bin, but I was always aware that what I liked was the pleasant society rather than the actual surroundings. These screwball repositories are built for utility, not comfort. There is a bleakness about their interiors which might exercise a depressing effect if you had not the conversation of dormitory 309 to divert your thoughts. The walls are bare, and when you go in or out you climb or descend echoing stairs. And the bars on the windows lower your spirits till you stop noticing them.
>
> All the windows at Tost were heavily barred, even those of the dining-room, though why the most unbalanced lunatic should want to get out of a dining-room by the window when the door was at his disposal, I cannot say. The gratifying result of this was to cause me take a step up in the animal kingdom. At Huy I had

felt like a water beetle. At Tost my emotions were more those of one of the residents of a Monkey House at the Zoo. If I had had a perch to swing on and somebody outside pushing nuts through the bars, the illusion would have been perfect.

And should one be passing through, Plum rather helpfully fills in for us the surrounding geography.

At first sight, Tost looks as if it were near nothing, except possibly the North Pole, but actually it is but a stone's throw from Slupska, Koppienitz, Peisketscham and Pnibw.

Given the situation, then, it seemed logical to Plum to curl up in his padded cell, and bang away at *Money in the Bank.* He was to be at Tost for nine months. Perhaps due to the fact that he was a celebrity, the Germans offered him quite a few special privileges during his stay, but it must have permeated through even Plum's naivety that it would not be wise to accept them, and he did not. There is also the fact, of course, that he had never attached much importance to privilege; and anyway, his padded cell he found really quite comfortable. This steadfast refusal of special treatment was written about by a correspondent for Associated Press, who in December 1940 visited the Tost asylum, where he talked with Plum. When the article hit America, his friends reacted immediately, for no-one had known of Wodehouse's whereabouts for over a year. Guy Bolton, possibly misguidedly, got up a petition for his immediate release, demanding that P.G. be sent back to America. It is true that America was not yet in the War, but the request was not totally logical, as Plum was British and not a citizen of the United States. An academic point, as it turned out, for Germany, other than issuing a bulletin testifying to Plum's continuing comfort and health, did nothing.

On the 21st of June 1941, however, P.G. was granted conditional freedom. This meant that he was to be released from Tost, and moved to the Hotel Adlon in Berlin, where he could remain under surveillance. The Adlon was the official German Foreign Office hotel, and was used in much the same way as the French and British governments used the Bristol in Paris and Claridges in London. It seems, though, that the Adlon was selected merely because it had rooms available at the time, while all others were full. Ethel, who had been living in France, immediately joined him at the Adlon, and within five days P.G. was broadcasting on the radio, from Berlin. These are the simple facts, and they resulted in an explosion. Many questions have to be answered here, however, the most notable being: Why was Wodehouse released from Tost? Why did he broadcast from Berlin? Why was the reaction to these broadcasts so hostile, and the effects so lasting? And what, exactly, did he say?

It is true that internees were automatically released at the age of sixty, and at this time P.G. was only four months off this age. It does not tally with what we know of

Ethel Wodehouse, with the ubiquitous Peke.

German wartime thinking, though, for them to shrug off four months. Precision from Germany we have come to expect. It is possible that he was released due to Guy Bolton's petition, which had been signed by quite a few United States Senators, but in that case the Germans probably would not have waited six months to do it. Was there then a link between the events of his release and his Berlin broadcasts which followed so soon afterwards? This seems likely, though not in the sense that his critics have imagined. If P.G. was released on condition he broadcast, why would he have accepted? He was, by his own admission, quite comfortable at Tost. To answer this, we must also bear in mind Ethel's almost simultaneous arrival in Berlin. If any 'pressure' was brought to bear on P.G., it was almost surely only in this form: it is possible that he was offered a reunion with his wife. This in no way suggests that he 'bought' his freedom, for this would have been granted anyway after four months. The truth is, P.G. welcomed the chance to broadcast to America, seeing such action as the perfect way of reassuring his friends and fans that he was alive and well – and if this meant he would also see his beloved Ethel again, then this was so much more to the good. The scripts, of course, were to be written by him, and not provided by the Germans. Wodehouse could see no dark plot hatching around him; he could not see what ulterior motive the Germans could have in commissioning these broadcasts, provided that he himself retained control of what was actually said. Very few people even heard the broadcasts, and few more have since read the transcripts (they were published in *Encounter* in October and November 1954). They are, quite simply, pure Wodehouse. They are witty, and harmless. He called the series of talks *How to Be an Internee without Previous Training*, and in them he described the various journeys and camps he had undergone, He does not make light of the hardships, although characteristically he underplays his own discomfort. The Germans he paints as people doing a job, and quite often messing it up. It is possibly only this to which people in wartime could have taken exception; he did not hate. It is hard to understand now, but for so prominent an Englishman not to hate his captors was seen as tantamount to siding with them. Wodehouse was denounced as a traitor.

Germany did not come out too well from the broadcasts, so why did they instigate them? It seems highly possible that they divined the reactions of the Western press. Lord Haw-Haw was much in the news, and the Germans might have known that the mere fact that P.G. Wodehouse had broadcast from Berlin would be enough to shock and demoralize Britain; it did not matter what he said. Germany might have seen this, but Wodehouse did not. This is the extent of his misdemeanour. He foolishly failed to foresee any of it, and although he saw himself as 'loony' much later in his life he admitted that he had taken ten whole years to realize what an ass he had been. He calls himself an ass, and this seems fair; naive he most certainly was. Any allegations of his having 'motives' or of being treacherous to his country are quite unfounded and ridiculous. This is the friendly and genuine ending to the series of broadcasts:

With this talk, I bring to an end the story of my adventures as British Civilian Prisoner Number 796, and before concluding I should like once more to thank all the kind people in America who wrote me letters while I was in camp. Nobody who has not been in a prison camp can realize what letters, especially letters like those I received, mean to an internee.

The torrent of anger in the British press that followed the broadcasts, then, was directed very much at the fact that Wodehouse had spoken on German radio, rather than at what he had said; the very word 'Berlin' was hateful to many Britons at the time. In under a month, a fierce and vile broadcast went out on the BBC. It was made by William Connor ('Cassandra', of the Daily Mirror) at the insistence of Duff Cooper, then the Minister of Information.

The 'information' contained in this invective was inaccurate, spiteful and slanderous, and it went out just after the nine o'clock news to an audience of millions, most of whom had previously heard nothing at all of the situation. As it was broadcast on the BBC, the speech was largely accepted, though some of the rhetoric employed seems to quite defy belief. Connor told the nation of 'a rich man trying to

Attacker : William Connor (alias Cassandra of the Daily Mirror)

make his last and greatest sale – that of his own country'. P.G. was referred to, incredibly, as a 'rich playboy' who pawned his honour to the Nazis 'for the price of a soft bed'. At the time of his internment Wodehouse was, of course, 'throwing a cocktail party'. 'Thirty pieces of silver' came up a little later, and the tirade ended cruelly with a description of an air-raid on P.G.'s beloved Dulwich, Although the people of Britain had heard not one word of any of Wodehouse's five broadcasts, the very firm impression given by Connor and Duff Cooper was that the man had been doing precisely the same as Lord Haw-Haw himself. Interestingly, the entry 'Wodehouse, P.G.' is notably absent from the Index to Duff Cooper's own memoirs, a volume entitled *Old Men Forget*.

Wodehouse himself, of course, was quite unaware of these attacks on him in England, and also of the fact that his friends, such as Denis Mackail, were striving to defend him. In America, where the broadcasts were actually received, the reaction could not have been more different. *The Saturday Evening Post* happily published *Money in the Bank*, and Doubleday put it out in book form in 1942. The broadcasts themselves were actually used by the U.S. War Department as models of anti-Nazi propaganda. These facts illustrate the truth. America was not yet a part of the War, and they did not yet hate. The senses of the British people were very close to the surface, and they over-reacted.

It was not until that Christmas that P.G. learned of the furore in Britain. He was incredulous, and quite totally horrified. He immediately strove to clarify the position and stress his loyalty to Britain, via the Swiss Embassy in Berlin, and he also applied for permission to return to England to explain in person. This request the Germans, quite naturally, refused. It was not in their interests to have the situation explained. Wodehouse had been foolish, and he was already living with his mistake.

He and Ethel spent the summers of 1942 and 1943 in the German countryside, financed by the monthly remittance from *The Saturday Evening Post*. For the rest of the year they were in Berlin. From there, P.G. wrote to Townend. 'Of course I ought to have had the sense to see that it was a loony thing to do to use the German radio for even the most harmless stuff, but I didn't. I suppose prison life saps the intellect.'

For two years, P.G. wrote, and completed two novels. Late in 1943, the Germans moved Plum and Ethel to Paris. Berlin was undergoing increased air-raids, and surveillance of the Wodehouses was becoming difficult. They were installed in the Hotel Bristol, and they were still there when the city was liberated the following summer. P.G. Wodehouse was very, very low at this time, for the news of a totally unpredicted and terrible tragedy had very recently reached him. His stepdaughter Leonora had died, at the age of thirty-nine. She had undergone a quite minor gynaecological operation, and had died under anaesthetic. The Wodehouses were stunned and grief-striken for months. P.G. had possibly been more fond of Leonora than of anyone else in the world.

This was a painful and difficult time for Wodehouse. He learned too that his mother had died in Surrey three years earlier, at the age of eighty-eight. Of course, this news did not affect him nearly so much as the death of Leonora, for he had hardly known his mother. Nonetheless, the clouds were continuing to gather. Now that Paris had been liberated, he knew too that his position with regard to the broadcasts would finally have to be sorted out. He reported to the victorious Americans, who contacted the British government, whereupon an official from the Home Office was sent out to make a full report. Wodehouse by now desperately wished to return to England and personally explain the whole situation, but this, he was told rather ominously, would not be wise. He had to content himself with co-operating with the investigation.

At this time, Malcolm Muggeridge was stationed in Paris with Intelligence; and was offered the job of 'keeping an eye on P.G. Wodehouse'. He agreed, he tells us in his autobiography,

> . . . with indecent alacrity; not because I was an ardent Wodehouse reader, or even because of a burning desire to make up for the shabby treatment he had indubitably received at the hands of his fellow-writers at the time of his notorious broadcasts from Berlin, but, primarily, out of curiosity, to see just how he had reacted to suddenly becoming a national villain after having been for so many years a national hero, or class totem.

Muggeridge went along to the Bristol, where he found Wodehouse 'a large, bald amiable-looking man, wearing grey flannel trousers, a loose sports jacket and what I imagine were golfing shoes, and smoking a pipe; a sort of schoolmaster's rig.' He seemed 'perfectly at ease.'

Muggeridge had many talks with P.G. over the next few days, and gradually pieced together the whole story of the broadcasts. He came to the conclusion that Wodehouse was released from Tost a few months before his sixtieth birthday 'as a result of well-meant but ill-advised representation by American friends.' Of the broadcasts themselves, Muggeridge recalls that they were

> . . . gone through minutely by more expert eyes than mine, but no-one has ever been able to find them other than blameless. They are, like everything Wodehouse writes, accomplished; . . . the broadcasts, in point of fact, are neither anti- nor pro-German, but just Wodehousian. He is a man singularly ill-fitted to live in a time of idealogical conflict, having no feelings of hatred about anyone, and no very strong views about anything. In the behaviour of his fellow humans, whoever they may be, he detects nothing more pernicious than a kind of sublime idiocy, and in commenting on public affairs rarely goes further than expressing the hope that

One of the last known pictures of Plum and Leonora together.

this or that august personage might be induced to return to his padded cell. I never heard him speak bitterly about anyone – not even about old friends who turned against him in distress. Such a temperament does not make for good citizenship in the second half of the Twentieth Century.

Muggeridge became very fond of Wodehouse. Of Ethel he wrote:

A bad sleeper, accustomed to wander about during the night, polishing tables and planning to pull down whatever house they happened to be occupying and re-build it nearer to her heart's desire; a mixture of Mistress Quickly and Florence Nightingale, with a touch of Lady Macbeth thrown in – I grew to love her.

On his return to London, Muggeridge had agreed to two favours. One was to procure for P.G. some tobacco, and the other to learn of the sales progress of P.G.'s books, in the light of events. A quantity of Three Nuns was duly acquired, though it is unclear whether this was the brand specified by P.G., or simply what was available in wartime London. (A personal and recent inspection of P.G.'s tobacco pouches revealed to me a mixture of Virginia and cigar leaf). A.P. Watt., Wodehouse's London agent, was at first reluctant to make any disclosure at all with regard to P.G.'s sales, but having assured himself that Muggeridge was on Plum's side he confided that the books were selling better than ever. The Englishman's reading taste was not to be swung by a few hysterical Members of Parliament or pressmen.

Muggeridge was pleased to have this news to relay to Plum, but almost immediately upon his return to Paris he learned that the Wodehouses had been arrested by the Paris police. According to Muggeridge,

. . . it seemed that at a dinner party given by the then *Préfet de Police*, Luiset, an English guest had remarked on how scandalous it was that two such notorious traitors as the Wodehouses should be at large in Paris; whereupon Luiset gave orders there and then that they should be arrested, and four men with sub-machine guns and wearing black leather jackets duly appeared in their bedroom at the Bristol Hotel and took them off.

Apart from the fact that the Wodehouses had by now been moved to the Lincoln Hotel, this appears to be more or less what happened, though the four thugs fail to make an appearance in P.G.'s own retelling of the incident to Townend.

My arrest came as a complete surprise. I have it from what is usually called a 'well-informed source' that an English woman was dining with the Prefect of Police, and said to him 'Why don't you arrest P.G. Wodehouse?' He thought it a splendid idea and sent out the order over the coffee and liqueurs, with the result that I woke up at one o'clock in the morning of November 22nd to find an *Inspecteur* at my bedside.

Ally : Malcolm Muggeridge, pictured here assuming the Punch editorial chair.

Plum and Ethel in Paris in 1945, complete with the Royal typewriter that replaced the old Monarch.

The upshot of it was that Plum and Ethel were both taken to the *Palais de Justice*, where they spent sixteen hours on wooden chairs in a draughty corridor. 'Aren't women wonderful?' P.G. wrote. 'Ethel took the whole thing in her stride without a word of complaint. She was simply magnificent, and the love and admiration which she has inspired in me for the last thirty years hit a new high.'

Naturally enough, no-one had the slightest idea why they had been arrested. Another official was flown out from England to sort out the situation. The British assumption was that the Wodehouses had broken some French laws, but the French seemed to imagine they were doing England a favour by locking them up. It was a mess. Muggeridge smoothed things over a bit, and the atmosphere became less hostile. Wodehouse wrote: 'We were given beds, and Malcolm Muggeridge – what a pal that man has been! – arrived loaded with bread, corned beef, champagne and cigars, and we had a banquet.'

The following day, Ethel was released. P.G. worked on a novel. After four days, he was removed to a hospital, not because he was ill, but because it seemed a fairly handy place to put him while the French and English authorities thrashed out the question of why he was being held in the first place. He was comfortable in the hospital and he was given everything he needed. 'It isn't a bad sort of life, if you have a novel to write', he said to Townend. And of course, P.G. did have a novel to write, *Uncle Dynamite* by name. He had been working on it in the *Palais de Justice* and he continued in the hospital, under the admiring eyes of the French police. In a letter to Townend, he talks of this Gallic awe; 'Seeing me hammering out my wholesome fiction, the *Inspecteurs* treat me with reverence. For two pins *(épingles)* they would call me *"Maître"*.'

None of it could put him off his stroke, however. As he wrote a few months later:

I have become very interested in Shakespeare, and am reading books about him, having joined the American Library here. A thing I can never understand is why all the critics seem to assume that his plays are a reflection of his personal moods and dictated by the circumstances of his private life. You know the sort of thing I mean. They say Timon of Athens is a pretty gloomy piece of work, which means that Shakespeare must have been having a rotten time when he wrote it. I can't see it. Do you find that your private life affects your work? I don't.

Of *Uncle Dynamite* he wrote: 'When I finish this one, I shall have five novels which have not been published in England, also ten short stories. I wonder if they ever will be published.' The other four were *Money in the Bank*, *Joy in the Morning*, *Full Moon* and *Spring Fever*.

The feeling in England was clearly worrying Wodehouse, and his continued frustration at being unable to cross the Channel and explain was growing hugely. If he genuinely believed that England would never again publish him, a few months later he was philosophizing over the situation.

> But it's a funny thing about writing. If you are a writer by nature, I don't believe you write for money or fame or even for publication, but simply for the pleasure of turning out the stuff. I really don't care much if these books are published or not. The great thing is that I've got them down on paper, and can read and re-read them and change an adjective for a better one and cut out dead lines.

In England, the 'affair' had by no means been settled. A barrister working for MI5 was despatched to Paris, and once more the entire business was gone through in detail. Questions, meanwhile, were being asked in the House of Commons, notably by Quintin Hogg, who felt a legal principle must surely be at stake, due simply to the fact that Wodehouse had broadcast on enemy radio during wartime, regardless of what was said. It was learned, however, that this bare action could not in itself be considered a criminal offence. The debating continued over the months. MI5 found that Wodehouse had been guilty only of foolishness, though as the dossier in question has been placed under the hundred-year rule, it is impossible to quote the wording of their findings. Early in 1945, the announcement came from the Rt Hon. Sir Anthony Eden that P.G. Wodehouse would face no charges, for he had broken no laws. The official view was clear, though still the MI5 barrister advised P.G. not to return to England. This wounded and puzzled him for years afterwards.

The release from the hospital now came through, and Malcolm Muggeridge installed the Wodehouses in a hotel in Barbizon. They were soon able to return to Paris, and rent a furnished flat. Life was at last beginning to return to normality, though P.G. himself, of course, had remained normal throughout, as an extract from a letter to Townend shows:

> I was thrilled by what you told me about Dulwich winning all its school matches last cricket season, including Harrow and Malvern. It's odd, but I don't find that world cataclysms and my own personal problems make any difference to my feelings about Dulwich.

It seems that Dulwich, however, had rather altered their feelings about him, though possibly the following letter which was published in *The Alleynian*, the school magazine, in July 1945, set the record straight again. It is an important letter, not least for the fact that for the first time it seemed to be dawning upon Wodehouse that the Germans might after all have had some ulterior motive in allowing him to broadcast, for he says for the first and only time that he was 'tricked'. The letter also very clearly sets out his innocence and his openness.

A gaunt and rather sombre Wodehouse in Paris at the end of the War, in 1945.

Defender : the author and critic George Orwell.

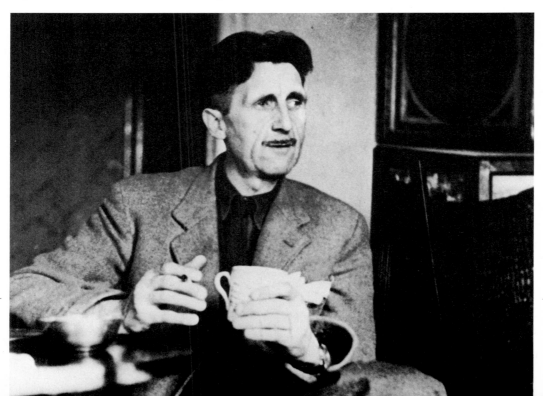

Mr P.G. Wodehouse

To the Editor, "The Alleynian"

Sir,

I have received from Mr P.G. Wodehouse a letter which is too long for publication in full. But extracts from it might interest your readers. It begins:

'I had a letter from Bill Townend a few days ago, handing me on the gist of a letter which you wrote to him regarding the feeling at Dulwich about me. He writes: "Rees says he feels you ought to know that Dulwich opinion regarding the broadcasts is very critical, even hostile, because the general idea is that you were persuaded to broadcast by the Nazis in order to add interest to their propaganda in return for some measure of liberty, and that what is needed is a brief account of what actually happened."

'I don't know if you have read a book by Harry Flannery called – I think – *Berlin Assignment*, in which he states that a representative of the German propaganda office came to see me in camp and arranged with me that I should be released in order to broadcast. This is absolutely untrue. I never received such a visit, nor was I ever approached on the matter. It was not until after my release that the subject of broadcasting came up.

'What happened was this. I was released on June 21, 1941, a few months before I was sixty. I should have been released automatically on reaching the age of sixty, and I imagine that I was given my freedom a little earlier because of the agitation which had been going on in America for my release.'

Mr. Wodehouse gives instances of this agitation, and proceeds:

'On arrival in Berlin I ran into a very old friend of mine, a German who had been at Hollywood with me. I was telling him about life in camp, and a friend of his, who joined us, suggested that I might like to broadcast an account of my experiences to my American readers. It was so exactly what I wanted to do that I jumped at the idea. All through the last ten months of my internment I had been receiving letters from American readers, very anxious to know how I was getting on and I had not been able to answer any of these, as in camp you are allowed to write only to near relatives. I felt that these people, not knowing the circumstances, would be thinking me ungrateful and ungracious for ignoring their letters, and it seemed to me that by broadcasting my experiences I could make a sort of interim acknowledgment. I can honestly say that it never occurred to me for a moment that there was anything wrong in using the German radio as a medium for getting in touch with people in America to whom I was very grateful. (Some of them had sent me parcels.) I can see now, of course, how idiotic it was of me to do such a thing and I naturally regret it very much, but at the time it never struck me that I was doing anything wrong.

'While in camp I had roughed out a humourous book about camp life, and I condensed this material into five talks, covering the five phases of my internment –

the first week in Loos prison, the second week in Liege barracks, the next five weeks at Huy citadel and the rest of the time at Tost in Upper Silesia, starting with a description of my arrest at Le Touquet. I recorded these talks on wax and went off to stay in the country and thought no more about it. It was only when my wife arrived in Berlin on July 28, just after the last talk had been broadcast, that I heard of the reaction in England.

"I see now, of course, that I was tricked into making these talks, and I naturally feel a damned fool, but I hope I have made it clear that there was never anything in the nature of a bargain with the Germans. I was released before there was any suggestion of a broadcast, and there was never any idea that my freedom was dependant on my broadcasting.

'This, fortunately, I can prove. Just after my last talk I received a cable from the editor of *The Saturday Evening Post*, who was considering for serial publication my novel *Money in the Bank*, which I had written in camp. He said he liked the story and was anxious to buy it, but could do so only on my giving him my assurance that I would stop talking on the German radio. I replied that I had already stopped, that I had never intended to do more than these five humorous descriptions of camp life and that he could be perfectly easy in his mind, as I would not speak again on any subject whatsoever. A week or so later I heard from him that he had bought the story, and it started running as a serial in November.

"Now this cable of mine, of which I have given you the gist, was handed to an official of the *Wilhelmstrasse* and sent off by him, and if there had ever been any idea that I had been released because of an agreement on my part to broadcast German propaganda, I hardly think the German authorities would have made no protest when I announced that I was through after giving five talks mostly about how I read Shakespeare while in camp and how internees who had no tobacco smoked tea. If I had made such an agreement they would undoubtedly have tried to hold me to it and sent me back to camp if I refused to carry it out. But they did nothing, and I went on living unmolested in the country. Eventually I was allowed to come to Paris.

'I gather there has been a great deal of indignation in England because I was supposed to be living at the Adlon Hotel, presumably at the expense of the German Government. I stayed at the Adlon for a month or two each winter because they would not let me stay anywhere else, and when there I paid all my own expenses. My wife got more than enough to pay our way through the sale of her jewellery. From early April till December each year we had no expenses as we were living in the country at the home of a relation of the Hollywood friend I mentioned earlier. When we came to Paris, I was able to get 350,000 francs from my Spanish publisher, and also to borrow from friends. I would never have been in Berlin at all, if it had been possible to go on living in the country. But the house there had to be closed during the winter on account of heating difficulties.

'While in Berlin, I hardly spoke to a German. I was very busy writing – I wrote three novels and ten short stories while in Germany – and our friends were a few English and American women married to or the widows of Germans.'

Mr. Wodehouse says that he has already given this account to Government Officials, but he would like to have the main facts published in *The Alleynian*.

I am, Sir, Yours, etc.,

R.T. REES.

Wodehouse had begun to clear his name, but in a very limited way, for his editors and publishers had advised silence as the best policy. His only other public announcement was in a letter to *Variety*, in which once more he sets forth the facts. Others were now springing to his defence, trying to finally make it clear to the world that such defence was not a whitewashing of Wodehouse's actions, nor an excuse for Wodehouse's actions, but a repetition of the truth that Wodehouse *had not done anything wrong*. The most notable essay came from George Orwell, his 'In Defence of P.G. Wodehouse'.

Muggeridge had introduced Orwell to Wodehouse in Paris. At first, P.G. had found him a 'gloomy sort of chap', though by 1946 he was writing to Townend that he 'liked him very much indeed', although he was not above mild reprimand. In another letter to Townend in 1946, P.G. wrote:

I wish these critics wouldn't distort facts in order to make a point. George Orwell calls my stuff Edwardian (which God knows it is. No argument about that, George) and says the reason for it being Edwardian is that I did not set foot in England for sixteen years and so lost touch with conditions there. Sixteen years, mark you, during most of which I was living in London and was known as Beau Wodehouse of Norfolk St. He is also apt to take some book which I wrote in 1907 and draw all sorts of portentous conclusions from it. Dash it, in 1907 I was practically in swaddling clothes, and it was extremely creditable to me that I could write at all. Still, a thoroughly nice chap, and we correspond regularly.

'In Defence of P.G. Wodehouse', though, was no distortion of facts, but a very clear *resumé* of what was, and what was imagined. Orwell wrote:

In the desperate circumstances of the time, it was excusable to be angry at what Wodehouse did, but to go on denouncing him three or four years later – and more, to let an impression remain that he acted with conscious treachery – is not excusable. . . . I suggest that it is now time to regard the incident as closed.

Interestingly, and characteristically, the point P.G. picked up from the essay, he relates to Townend:

Did you happen to see a thing by George Orwell entitled 'In Defence of P.G. Wodehouse?' He says that my indiscretion (the broadcasts) gave a good propaganda opening to the left-wingers in England because 'it was a chance to expose a wealthy parasite.' Has it ever occurred to you that that is how authors are regarded in England? You, me, Shakespeare, all of us, just parasites. (Have you read any good parasites lately?)

By now it was 1946, and *Money in the Bank* was to be published in England. P.G. was worried about its reception, for this, he felt, would be the first real tester as to how his followers now regarded him. Punch reviewed the book thus: 'Mr P.G. Wodehouse's latest is as brilliant as any of its predecessors. . . . The technique is as inimitable as Jeeves.' Compton Mackenzie wrote: 'The ingenious plot, the marvellous simile, the preposterous characters which come to life and remain alive, the continuously dynamic dialogue – here they all are again. Let us make the most of a writer who is *sui generis*.' Within a few weeks Jenkins had sold nearly 30,000 copies, and were reprinting. The message was neon: Welcome back, Plum. You have never been away.

However, gratifying though all this was, and despite the total exoneration of any guilt that had officially been granted Wodehouse, he still felt the need to appear in England and make the position crystal. Still he was discouraged by his advisors. It is hard to understand why such persistent advice was given. P.G., certainly, was bewildered by it, but possibly he thought that having innocently committed this one huge indiscretion, it might be better not to risk another; he bowed to the advice of his friends, and remained silent. It is unfortunate that the British press, who had given so much space and attention to the initial accusations, hardly mentioned the fact that the Wodehouse escutcheon was now officially blotless. To this day, the sort of person who dimly recalls having read a bit of Wodehouse 'at school' – this rather silly statement intended to imply, no doubt, that they have since progressed to infinitely more grown-up stuff – will also remember that there was 'something about him with the Germans during the War, was there not?' Mud, unfortunately, sticks.

Bill Townend's view of Plum may hardly be said to be impartial, but for the very fact that he knew and understood the man better than almost anyone, his opinion must be noted. Plum, he says, was one 'who had never in his life had a really unkind thought concerning any other human being.' To sum up these wartime incidents, then, it seems that P.G. had been found guilty only of innocence.

As Malcolm Muggeridge points out, though, Wodehouse more than did his bit in the War, for it appears that the Germans took his writings as a very literal guide to the English way of life. As a consequence of this, when one of their spies was picked up in a boggy field in the Fen country, he was found to be wearing not only a parachute, but also a pair of lavender spats. There is no official record, but it seems not impossible that this unfortunate and impeccably trained German might have regaled his captors with a 'Pip-pip!' or two – or even, dare we hope, a 'Vot-ho!'

P.G. WODEHOUSE
FULL MOON

P.G. WODEHOUSE
The Old Reliable

P.G. WODEHOUSE
BARMY IN WONDERLAND

P.G. WODEHOUSE
Cocktail Time

CHAPTER TEN

FULL MOON

Peace reigned in the butler's pantry. The sweet air of the summer evening poured in through the open window. It was as if Nature had blown the All Clear.
Blandings Castle was itself again.

'Crime Wave at Blandings' from LORD EMSWORTH AND OTHERS

It's funny about people who live in the city. They chuck out their chests, and talk about little old New York being good enough for them, and there's a street in heaven they call Broadway, and all the rest of it ; but it seems to me that what they really live for is that three weeks in the summer when they get away into the country.

'At Geisenheimer's' from THE MAN WITH TWO LEFT FEET

The Le Touquet house had declined into a near-ruin during the War, and was now up for sale. The Wodehouses were living in St Germain-en-Laye, which P.G. described as a 'heavenly place', nine miles out of Paris. He was, of course, writing, but he had his problems. 'Do you find you write more slowly than you used to?' he asked Townend in a letter. 'I don't know if it is because *The Mating Season* is a Jeeves story, and in a Jeeves story every line has to have some entertainment value, but I consider it a good day's work if I get three pages done. I remember I used to do eight a day regularly.'

There were even problems with books he had already written, due to the hang-over of rationing.

In *Joy in the Morning*, Bertie speaks of himself as eating a steak and Boko is described as having fried eggs for breakfast, and Grimsdick of Jenkins is very agitated about this, because he says the English public is so touchy about food that stuff like this will probably cause an uproar. I have changed the fried egg to a sardine and cut out the steak, so I hope the situation is saved. But I was reading Agatha Christie's *The Hollow* just now, presumably a 1946 story, and the people in it simply gorge roast duck and souffles and caramel cream and so on, besides having a butler, several parlourmaids, a kitchen maid and a cook. I must say it

Four first editions : Full Moon *(1947),* The Old Reliable *(1951),*
Barmy In Wonderland *(1952), and* Cocktail Time *(1958).*

encouraged me to read *The Hollow* and to see that Agatha is ignoring present conditions in England.

The year was 1946, and the plan was to return to America. However, Ethel needed new clothes, and went to Paris a lot; the Wodehouses finally set sail in 1947. P.G. had not seen America for ten years, and he received quite a welcome. The gentlemen of the press were very, very evident – on the ship when it docked, and later. Wodehouse recalled:

> My second morning I held a formal 'press conference' at the Doubleday offices, with a candid camera man taking surreptitious photographs all the time. These were the literary columnists. I am going to a cocktail party at the house of one of them next week.
>
> Next day I was interviewed on the radio, reaching 350 stations, and the day after that on television. All this sounds as if I were a hell of a celebrity, but the explanation is that Doubleday's publicity hound arranges it all in the hope that it will lead to the sale of a copy or two of *Joy in the Morning*. I don't suppose it helps a bit, really. I don't imagine the great public sits listening spellbound while I answer questions from the interlocutor, and says; 'My God! So that's Wodehouse! How intelligent he looks! What a noble brow! I must certainly buy that last book of his!' Much more probably they reach out and twiddle the knob and get another station.

If Fame had the slightest intention of going to his head and bowling him over, it was being pretty sluggardly about the whole thing.

Life was picking up. P.G.'s literary affairs were now in the hands of Scott Meredith, whom Wodehouse thought 'an amazing chap', and who was selling his stories to the likes of *Cosmopolitan* quite as if they were hot cakes. Doubleday and Jenkins were publishing away like the dickens, and Plum had resumed his old alliance with Guy Bolton. Towards the end of 1947, they were both working on an adaptation of a Sacha Guitry play, *Don't Listen Ladies*. Plum wrote on, his books selling better than ever, despite the changing times. Even he noticed occasionally that the world was evolving, as is the way with worlds. He wrote to Townend:

> I have sent you – at enormous expense, four dollars, no less – a book that has headed the American best-seller lists for months, *The Naked and the Dead* (by Norman Mailer). I can't give you a better idea of how things have changed over here than by submitting that novel to your notice. It's good, mind you – in fact, I found it absorbing – but isn't it incredible that you can print in a book nowadays stuff which when we were young was found only on the walls of public lavatories.

In 1949, he was lamenting the death of *The Strand*, the last of the great and famous English magazines. 'How on earth does a young writer of light fiction get going these

Arriving in New York, one of them displaying influences of Paris couture.

days?' he asked Townend, echoing the question of many a young writer of light fiction. Of the state of transatlantic journals, P.G. had this to say.

My considered opinion, after a careful study of today's American magazines, is that 90% of the editors are cuckoo. I think that when one of them applies for a job on a magazine, they ask him 'Any insanity in your family?' and if he says, 'You bet there is. My father thought he was Napoleon and nothing would convince my mother that she was not a tea-pot', they engage him at a large salary.

P.G. was adapting *Spring Fever* into a play. The adaptation proved to be so far removed from the original, however, that he decided, fairly naturally, to adapt the adaptation into a novel, and this he called *The Old Reliable*. Which he was. He also put his mind to adapting some other play that had been plonked in his lap, but he didn't enjoy the task. While summing up the play's qualities, he saw fit to quote James Thurber: 'It had only one fault. It was kind of lousy.'

Late in 1950 he was writing to Townend:

The night before last I was interviewed on the radio by none other than Mrs

American publication of Full Moon. *The manic grin and the uncharacteristic cigarette do not testify to an inner tranquillity.*

Franklin D. Roosevelt. A charming woman, and I would have liked to have lolled back in my chair afterwards and had a long and interesting conversation about life in the White House. Unfortunately she threw me out on my ear the moment the thing was over.

Plum met John Steinbeck the same evening, and politely enquired as to the prosperity of Steinbeck's new play, premièred that week. Steinbeck did not reply, for Steinbeck's new play had proved a disaster and had already come off. The bane of Plum's life, small talk.

Throughout his life, P.G. had been nothing if not fit, but a potentially serious situation arose the following year, when he reported having suffered 'a giddy attack'. He wrote unemotionally to Townend:

> . . . I have been taking every known form of test, and the general view is that I have got a tumour on the brain. If this is correct, it is presumably the finish, as I don't suppose I can survive a brain operation at my time of life.

Bill Townend must have been greatly relieved to receive P.G.'s next letter a week later, where he states: '. . . the docs have decided I have not got a tumour on the brain'. The docs then went on to suggest most other bits and pieces, notably the eyes, as the probable root cause of the giddiness. Plum kept tally: 'The score, then, to date is that I am deaf in the left ear, bald, subject to mysterious giddy fits and practically cock-eyed.'

P.G. seemed to recover his old vigour pretty rapidly after this little setback, though, and he wrote a few novels. Life in New York, howsomever, was becoming just a bit trying. Despite the fact that the Wodehouses' address was 1000 Park Avenue, unpleasant things happened.

> Life in New York continues jolly, but it would be much jollier if it wasn't for the ruddy Crime Wave. Practically everyone you meet is either coming away from sticking up a bank or just setting out to stick up a bank. . . last week Ethel was held up at a dressmaker's on Madison Avenue. She was in the middle of being fitted, when a man came in brandishing a large knife and asked for contributions. He got $18 off Ethel, and disappeared into the void.

The New York state might have had something to do with Plum's eagerness to accept Guy Bolton's offer of a collaboration on a play featuring Jeeves, for this would entail staying with Guy in the small town of Remsenburg, on Long Island. P.G. liked Remsenburg. Ethel liked Remsenburg. One morning she returned from one of her shopping trips having bought a house there, and was very soon supervising the alterations and decoration. She seems to have borne in mind Plum's modest tastes this time. Plum was all for it, and the play was fairly scudding along. It was called *Come on, Jeeves*, and was soon to be adapted into the novel *Ring for Jeeves*. Plots, after all, were valuable stuff.

Well, is it a bird? No, it's Sean O'Casey,
the man who dubbed Wodehouse 'Performing Flea'.

Inspired by the success of this most recent collaboration, P.G. and Guy plunged into their memoirs of the golden days of the musical, *Bring on the Girls*. The English edition was considerably revised, as Jenkins considered the original version to be over-concerned with America. More 'autobiography' was on the way, when Bill Townend sent Wodehouse 200,000 words of Plum's own writing – his correspondence over the years – with the suggestion that these might make quite a good book. P.G. cut and polished a fair deal, and the result was published under the title *Performing Flea*. To make this choice of title clearer, P.G. wrote:

With Sean O'Casey's statement that I am 'English literature's performing flea', I scarcely know how to deal. Thinking it over, I believe he meant it to be complimentary, for all the performing fleas I have met have impressed me with their sterling artistry and that indefinable something which makes the good trouper.

About this time, too, P.G. yielded to buying a television.

What a loathsome invention it is. You hear people say it's going to wipe out books, theatres, radio and motion pictures, but I wonder. I don't see how they can help running out of material eventually. The stuff they dish out is bad enough now, and will presumably get worse. (Not that you can go by what I predict. I was the man who told David Graham Bell not to expect too much of that thing he had invented called the telephone or some such name, as it could never be more than an amusing toy.)

P.G. was now seventy-two, and working like blazes. *Jeeves and the Feudal Spirit* skittered off the pen, and *French Leave* rapidly followed. Plum's old friend Malcolm Muggeridge had now become the editor of *Punch*, and P.G. eagerly set to some articles for him. Everything in the garden could be said to be, at the very least, rosy. Perfection was soon attained, in Plum's view, when the house in Remsenburg became the permanent Wodehouse home, instead of merely a summer residence as had been its role to date. New York was no longer.

The next step was a book called *America, I Like You*. This was again autobiographical-ish, and based on the *Punch* articles. Herbert Jenkins, of course, were not bowled over by the title, and a revised edition was published in England as *Over Seventy*. Plum's original title seems to have gone to his head, however. He had been living in America for a long time, and in 1955 it appeared natural to him to be naturalized. He formally adopted United States citizenship.

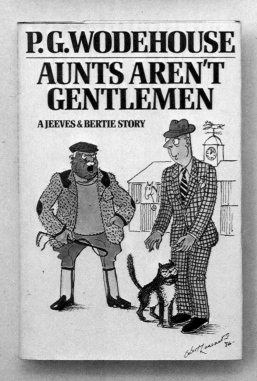

CHAPTER ELEVEN

THE OLD RELIABLE

He was humming as he approached the terrace. He had his programme all mapped out. For perhaps an hour, till the day had cooled off a little, he would read a Pig book in the library. After that he would go and take a sniff at a rose or two and possibly do a bit of snailing. These mild pleasures were all his simple soul demanded. He wanted nothing more. Just the quiet life, with nobody to fuss him.

'Crime Wave at Blandings' from LORD EMSWORTH AND OTHERS

I
rom this time on, the truth in Plum's own *resumé* of his existence becomes very evident. 'Just writing one book after another', he said, 'that's my life.' Each and every Christmas, the British and American fans were treated to 'the new Wodehouse', and all was serene – until 1959, when once again he suffered a giddy spell. This seemed rather more worrying than the last, which had been worrying enough, for now Plum found that he could not walk properly, and was therefore confined to bed. In 1951, at the time of his first attack, he conveyed to Townend the medical advice he had received: 'My doctor, by the way, summing up on the subject of the giddy fits and confessing his inability to explain them, said, "Well, if you have any more, you'd better just *have* them." I said I would.' And so he did. It has been observed before that it is dashed difficult to keep a good man down; P.G., of course, was very good indeed, and therefore it is only mildly surprising to learn that a couple of weeks later he was up and about, and writing a book.

It was around this time too that the globe at large decided that by now Plum was a Grand Old Man of Letters. He was elected to the Punch Table, but never made the trip to England to carve his initials in the woodwork, such being the custom, rather like the handprints outside Grauman's Chinese Theatre, though infinitely more civilized and, naturally enough, select. In 1961 he celebrated his eightieth birthday, and the post offices of the world had a field day with the telegrams. *Ice in the Bedroom* appeared, in a vile dust-wrapper, though that of *Wodehouse at Work* made up for it, bearing as it did the Low caricature of Plum. The appearance of this first

Four first editions : A Pelican at Blandings *(1969),* Much Obliged, Jeeves *(1971),*
Aunts Aren't Gentlemen *(1974), and* Sunset at Blandings *(1977).*

critical work rather flattered P.G., though this was tempered by mild amazement that 'a certain learned Usborne' should go into his stuff in such detail. The book was by no means a dry and deadly study, however, as were one or two later American works, but it jollied along spiffingly, conveying a great respect and admiration for Plum, as well as an intimate knowledge of the books. It was revised and updated in 1977.

All the newspapers and magazines wanted interviews with the Great Man, and he obliged. No, he didn't go to parties. No, he didn't go to New York. He did exercises, walked his dogs, read a great deal, watched appalling soap-operas on afternoon television, and – needless to say – he wrote. And wrote. And really nothing disturbed the pattern for years except the death of his very old friend and correspondent Bill Townend, in 1962. Wodehouse was very affected by this and he felt the loss keenly.

By 1965, P.G.'s work had come to the small screen, and was being published in *Playboy*. Most people seemed delighted about all this, but Plum himself merely tolerated the situation. In a *Sunday Times* interview with Philip Norman, he confided that in his opinion Ian Carmichael came over only as a middle-aged burlesque of Bertie (who was always meant to be twenty-fivish) and Dennis Price's Jeeves Plum found rather pasty-faced. However, he has also expressed a totally opposite view to this, so we can only assume that he was at best indifferent.

LEFT: *P.G. at home in Long Island, swinging from the hip. The swivel chair and desk in the background are now in the P.G.W. Corner in Dulwich College.*

BELOW: *Wodehouse at work. He is now approaching his nineties and seems to have come to terms with the electric typewriter.*

RIGHT: *Dennis Price imitating the Inimitable. Another scene from 'Jeeves and the Greasy Bird'.*

FAR RIGHT: *Bertie and Sippy in the Bow Street dock, following a night of razzle-dazzle. From 'Jeeves and the Stand-In for Sippy' (BBC 1967).*

FAR RIGHT, BELOW: *Young Man in Spats. Ian Carmichael as Bertie Wooster in a scene from 'Jeeves and the Greasy Bird' – one of the World of Wooster series broadcast by the BBC in 1967.*

BELOW: *Ian Carmichael as a monocled Wooster, don't you know.*

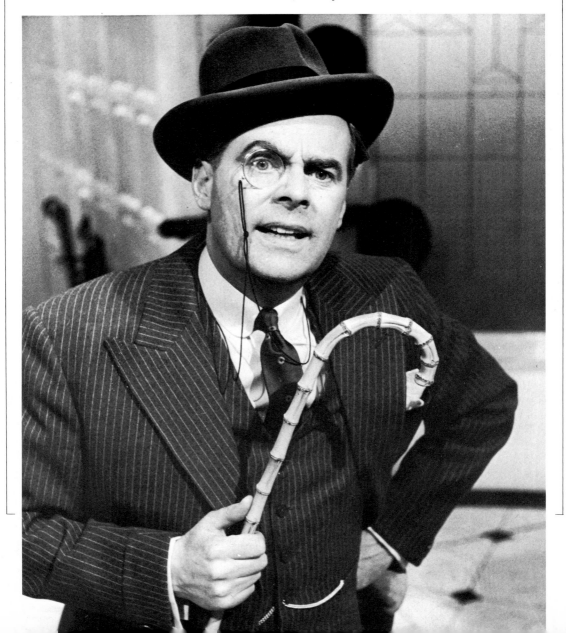

*Ukridge (Anton Rodgers) is sitting on the lavatory, and Corky (Julian Holloway)
is soaping Pekes with a vengeance. A scene from the BBC Ukridge series.*

The *Playboy* thing didn't delight him either. He said:

It makes an awful difference having no magazines to write for. Of course, I do
have things published in *Playboy*. They've published all my latest stories, the last
dozen or so, but they take such a time using them. I never like the way they look in
Playboy at all. I hate a fussed-up magazine like that; half the page devoted to a
naked girl, a bit to your story.

A slight exaggeration this view, actually, but it does raise a couple of points, if that's
the word.

Despite Plum's opinion of the Wooster TV programmes, though, the public liked
them, and they were very successful. Never ones to let a good thing die, the Corporation charged on with a fresh series called *Blandings Castle*, with Ralph
Richardson, and then Ukridge, starring Anton Rodgers. Neither quite duplicated
the success of the Jeeves lot, however, and no more was seen of P.G. on TV until the

*Sir Ralph Richardson as Lord Emsworth with Jack Radcliffe as McAllister
and some unidentified sow as the Empress. From 'Blandings Castle' (BBC).*

mid-seventies, when John Alderton and Pauline Collins brought the Wodehouse Playhouse to the screen. Alderton recalls that when Plum was approached with a list of Mulliner stories intended to form the basis of the series, P.G. excused himself from the room in order to read them. An occasional guffaw could be heard from next door. Soon he emerged, grinning. Yes indeed, he agreed, 'Some of them are *awfully* good.' He introduced each play himself, somewhat slurrily it is true, and the finished products were the most successful transference of the golden words to film. Even Plum approved.

LEFT: *Adrian Mulliner, detective extraordinary, trying hard to demonstrate that it is 'The Smile that wins' (1978).*

BELOW: *John Alderton and Pauline Collins unveil 'The Truth about George'– Wodehouse Playhouse (1975).*

John Alderton as Smallwood Bessimer in the BBC Wodehouse Playhouse production 'Tangled Hearts' (1978).

*A relaxed Plum
and a reflective Ethel
toast each other
with Dry Martinis
on the terrace
of their Long Island
home.*

He saw out the sixties by writing books and seeing to the P.G. Wodehouse Center which he had set up on Long Island – a sanctuary for stray dogs and cats, financed by himself. Next to Life, he loved animals.

Ethel was over eighty by now, but she still ferried Plum around in a scarlet Buick, and she still made good, strong and ice-cold Martinis. Her main concern was that it was now impossible to find servants, a concern not shared by Plum, whose view of servants was summed up when he announced 'I hate having my things messed around.' Of his writing at this time he said: 'I always get the feeling in between books that I'll never get another plot, but I always do; I've felt that for about fifty years.' He still saw a lot of Guy Bolton, and he still watched horrid serials on television. He also made a point of replying personally to each of the many fan letters that rolled in from all over the place; he even posted the replies himself.

Wodehouse's ninetieth birthday was an international literary event, and a new Jeeves novel was published both in England and in America on the actual day – 15th of October, 1971. At this time, the rumour went around London that P.G. would actually be making the trip to join in the celebrations, but the journey never materialized.

And so P.G. Wodehouse, now commencing his hundredth decade, plunged into the nineteen-seventies, and wrote more books. Robert Robinson visited him on Long Island and interviewed him for the BBC Book Programme. The interviewer had some difficulty in restraining Plum from being disarmingly flattering about Robinson's own books, though finally elicited some information about Wodehouse, now aged ninety-three.

ROBINSON: How do you spend your day, Mr Wodehouse – how do you plan it out?

P.G.W.: Well, I get up awfully early, have my breakfast about quarter past eight, and then I generally work after breakfast. When I've got any work to do, when I'm doing a novel, I always give up the morning to it. And then, after lunch, Ethel and I go out to pick up the mail, take the two dogs down to the water, run them around, and get back here about five o'clock. After that, I just read.

ROBINSON: Do you keep to a strict writing schedule when you're working on a novel?

P.G.W.: No, I don't think so. I like to do some work every day, but the sort of novel I write depends so much on when you get an idea for a scene. If you've got the idea, then it's easy to write the scene, so I don't tie myself down to any particular time.

ROBINSON: Do you work it all out beforehand?

Plum, introducing an episode of the BBC Wodehouse Playhouse.
The photograph was taken in 1975, one week before his death.

P.G.W.:   Very much so. About four hundred pages of notes. I write down every-
           thing that comes into my mind, and about half of it is about characters
           that aren't in the book at all. Do you find that you do that too?

Robinson blushes, and deftly bows out of this one. He then tackles Plum on the
question of a visit to England.

P.G.W.:   It's rather difficult, my legs have gone, you know. I don't know whether
           I could survive in the city any longer.
ROBINSON: Do you ever go to New York? You're not very far away.
P.G.W.:   Never. I haven't been for five years. I used to go quite a lot. Suddenly,
           about a year ago, I found walking awfully difficult. I have to walk with a
           stick – it's not so much that my legs aren't strong enough, the balance is
           all wrong. I was walking round this ground and suddenly I started
           toppling over the side, staggered for a pace or two, and then fell a
           frightful whack. So now I always use a stick.

All this made rather sad viewing. In addition, Plum's fingers were becoming
increasingly arthritic, permitting only the slow touching of the keys of an electric
typewriter. *Aunts Aren't Gentlemen* had just been published, however, and it did a
body a power of good to be reassured that the essential Wodehouse was still in
fighting form. It was a Jeeves and Bertie, and a corker.

A short time after this interview, in January 1975, the final honour was belatedly
bestowed upon Plum; he received a knighthood in the New Year Honours List,
along with Charles Chaplin. As *The Times* reported on the front page: 'The knighthood will be seen by many as official indication that he no longer languishes in the
shadows after the criticisms aimed at him during the Second World War when the
Nazis made propaganda out of his broadcasts from Berlin.' Although one has never
quite thought of P.G. as being over-given to 'languishing in shadows', one gets the
drift. Sad that 'official indication' had taken over thirty years in coming, but better
late, as they tend to say, than never. The Introduction to the 1931 *Jeeves Omnibus*
opens thus:

> The trackless desert of print which we see before us, winding on and on into
> the purple distance, represents my first Omnibus Book: and I must confess that,
> as I contemplate it, I cannot overcome a slight feeling of chestiness, just the faint
> beginning of that offensive conceit against which we authors have to guard so

ABOVE RIGHT: *Plum's ninetieth birthday celebrations in Riverhead, Long Island.*
A sad photograph, though. The hearing aid, the unfamiliar cigar between
hardened fingers, and Plum's distant gaze do not add up to a picture of revelry.

RIGHT: *The birthday party. Here, Plum tolerates being mothered by 'aunts'.*

carefully. I mean, it isn't everyone. . . . Well, dash it, you can't say it doesn't mark an epoch in a fellow's career and put him just a bit above the common herd. P.G. Wodehouse, OB. Not such a very distant step from P.G. Wodehouse, OM.

And indeed, forty-four years later, he came a jolly sight closer. It is true that on hearing of the KBE, Plum was honoured in every sense, but his sense of proportion, of course, was retained. *The Times* reported, via Reuter, 'Mr P.G. Wodehouse, who is too frail to travel to England, said today at his home on Long Island: "I may go to the British Embassy in Washington to receive the award. But I understand that all they do is pin a ribbon on you." '

The Times leader writer, though, positively gambolled with delight.

Charlie Chaplin and P.G. Wodehouse, one in his eighties, the other in his nineties, and with fair claims to be considered the funniest men in the world. If there is anyone else who has given as much amusement to as many people for as many years, then he too deserves a knighthood. . . It is sanity, not frivolity, to single out these comedians of genius at this gloomy time. Mr. Wodehouse certainly, and Mr. Chaplin possibly, would disclaim the possession of anything 'relevant' to say about our public predicament, though others might say it for them.

If a contemporary moral of some sort is required of their *oeuvres*, it is better to look for it in Mr. Chaplin's indomitable little man beset with adversity, and in Mr. Wodehouse's unfailing gaiety attached to an uncommon respect for the medium of his art, which is a sure, limpid, richly associative English prose.

The Times, then, along with everyone else, was pleased. One says everyone, but there could, I suppose, have been one or two unenlightened curmudgeons who did not share this pleasure. One tends to endorse Auberon Waugh's view on this, as expressed in the *New Statesman* the month after the knighthood.

I confess I find myself slightly shocked when anybody admits to not liking Wodehouse, although I can see that this is an unreasonable reaction. But I think I can be dogmatic on a few points from my own observation: that Wodehouse has been more read than any other English novelist by his fellow novelists; that nobody with any genuine feeling for the English language has failed to recognise

ABOVE LEFT: *A photograph taken on the 1st of January 1975, when the news of Plum's knighthood broke. The sword was a gift from his American agent and publisher.*

FAR LEFT: *The price of fame. Wodehouse is measured for a Madame Tussaud's waxwork. The sculptor is John Blakely, and the suspense is killing.*

LEFT: *And here it is. The finished thing. No, it's not Eisenhower – it's Wodehouse. Where, among other things, are the spectacles? Where indeed.*

at least an element of truth in Belloc's judgement of 1934, that Wodehouse was 'the best writer of English now alive, the head of my profession'; that the failure of literary academic criticism to take any account of Wodehouse's supreme mastery of the English language or the profound influence he has had on every worth-while English novelist in the past fifty years demonstrates in better and conciser form than anything else how the Eng. Lit. industry is divorced from the subject it claims to study.

This formed part of one of the many final and very evidently heartfelt tributes, for that week, on St Valentine's Day, Sir Pelham Grenville Wodehouse, LLD, had died. *The Times* printed a thirty-eight column-inch obituary, including the following paragraph:

> There was nothing of the literary man about Wodehouse. He might have been a retired master from Wrykyn, the public school of some of his best early stories. Dressed in blue blazer and grey flannel trousers, figure kept trim by golf, swimming and leading the simple life, he made no attempt to shine in any company.

No indeed; which goes some way to explain why he glowed so warm.

When Leonora died in 1944, a shocked Wodehouse had uttered: 'I thought she was immortal.' Plum is immortal. For as well as all the great characters we know and adore, can we not also at any time share the company of scores of lesser lights, who nonetheless shine so brightly? Chaps like Stiffy Byng or Stilton Cheesewright, Captain Cuthbert Gervase Brabazon-Biggar and Catsmeat Potter-Pirbright – Oofy Prosser, Gussie Fink-Nottle, Barmy Fotheringay-Phipps and Pongo Twistleton-Twistleton – to say nothing at all of Looney Coote and Dogface Rainsby.

No. The truth is, Plum didn't die at all; he just trickled off somewhere, for a breather.

P.G. Wodehouse: The Bee's Knees. And then some.

A picture taken very shortly before Plum's death.
He is savouring again the delights of The World of Mr. Mulliner.

I suppose I am the only man ... Frozen ... Even ... Corbett ... white ... ant forced in the 90's, after he was terrific. (Insert on t)

The thing I remember best about the book is that Dombey gave it a nasty review in the Spectator and Evelyn Waugh rushed to its defence and attacked the fellow with tooth and claw, starting a controversy which lasted for months. I have often wondered why more authors don't do this sort of thing, but it brightens up the whole issue of paper which need brightening up, besides giving the recipient of the stinker the comfortable feeling that he is not without friends and allies.

I suppose this book has defects, but I am lucky in not being able to detect them. I never can with my books. ... I like this book ... I like all my books. Others may not, but I do. When I have finished a book — and rewritten it and rewritten it again and polished up all the weak spots — I get a sort of cosy glow and the conviction that it's all right ... It seems to me that Nicholas Jules St Xavier Auguste, Marquis de Maufringneuse et Valentin — Molyneux is

From the mass of manuscript material bequeathed to Dulwich College.

COLLECTOR'S GUIDE

Two quotations from *Stiff Upper Lip, Jeeves*:

1. If a collector pinches something from another collector, it doesn't count as stealing.
2. Collectors are never pleased when they learn that a rival collector has acquired at an insignificant price an *objet d'art* of great value.

P.G., you might infer, didn't have a lot of time for collecting or collectors, tending to see one of these said collectors as some fanatical bimbo after a gristly cow-creamer, or similar, and willing to sacrifice life and limb (usually Bertie's) to get it. We book collectors are altogether more decorous, though. Aren't we. Anyway, there are an awful lot of Wodehouse collectors both in Britain and America, as well as in Japan and France – and all over the place, let's face it. The thing is, they are all after first editions in the dust-wrapper, and it is getting more and more difficult to find them. There is now almost no such thing as a 'common' title, for although the very early ones are still extremely scarce, even books of the forties, fifties and sixties are becoming rare in really fine condition. In my book *Collecting Modern First Editions* (Studio Vista, 1977), I concluded the P.G. entry thus: 'It ought to be remembered that these prices are rising all the time.' True, true, very true. They have risen like the dickens, and I see no reason why they should not continue to do so, for, as the firsts dry up, so more and more people become interested in acquiring them. Supply and demand, don't you know.

Now all this must make for bucking reading among those of you who have a complete collection of first editions, (are there such people? I am missing three, not including the plays). But for those of you just starting out, don't be dispirited! Well actually, you'd better be just a little dispirited in the light of what I've said, but even in these troubled, as they say, times you know, it ought to be possible to gather thirty or so without *too* much trouble, green stuff permitting.

Following this little essay, there is a bibliography of books which I believe to be complete, with descriptions of each title – including, for the first time, the all-important dust-wrappers – and all other relevant data (English and American publishers, dates, precedence, bindings, etc). This will leave you in no doubt as to what you are looking for, and I now propose to give a few hints as to what you might expect to pay for the things, always assuming that you can find them. This point, though obvious, must be borne in mind, for although I might estimate a certain book as being worth £25, there are far more people eager to part with the pony than there are copies of the book available. Why, then, should the book not be worth £30? No reason at all, actually. Tricky thing, pricing.

Nonetheless, the prices I am about to quote would be about right from dealers in the know, at the time of writing – *i.e.*, retail prices of decent copies in the dust-wrapper, where applicable. First, the code:

Grade A   Up to £5
Grade B   Up to £10
Grade C   Up to £15
Grade D   Up to £20
Grade E   Up to £30

There are quite a few titles, you will be discouraged to hear, that are worth a lot more than this. I'll try and give a more precise figure for these.

GRADE A: Nos 60, 107, 110, 111, 112, 113, 115, 116, 117, 118, 119, 120, 121, 122, 123, 124, 125, 126, 127, 129, 130.

GRADE B: Nos 28, 32, 33, 51, 56, 61, 64, 69, 72, 74, 75, 76, 79, 80, 81, 82, 83, 84, 85, 86, 87, 88, 89, 90, 91, 94, 97, 98, 99, 101, 102, 103, 104, 105, 106, 108, 109, 114, 128.

GRADE C: Nos 24, 26, 29, 34, 36, 37, 38, 39, 41, 42, 43, 44, 45, 46, 47, 49, 50, 52, 55, 57, 58, 59, 65, 66, 67, 68, 70, 71, 77, 78, 92, 93, 96.

GRADE D: Nos 25, 27, 30, 31, 35, 40, 48, 54, 62, 63, 73, 95, 100.

GRADE E: Nos 21, 53.

And now, the class stuff. This is very difficult to rate at all, it's so scarce. Soon after I estimated *The Pothunters* at 'up to £100' in *Collecting Modern First Editions*, an American collector offered me $500 for my own copy. So what is it worth? You see the point, don't you. All one can say, I think, is that Nos 1, 2, 3, 4, 6, 7, 8, 9, 10, 11, 12, 13, 15, 15(i), and 23 would be *at least* £100, and some very possibly twice that. Not that much farther behind would be Nos 5, 14, 16, 17, 18, 19, 20, and 22. Without doubt *the* most scarce titles are *The Pothunters, Love among the Chickens, Not George Washington, The Globe By the Way Book,* and *The Swoop.*

So now there is really nothing to stop anyone going out with armfuls of cash, soon to return home with buckets brimming with pristine goodies, very much as outlined above.

And good luck to you.

COMPLETE BIBLIOGRAPHY OF ENGLISH AND AMERICAN FIRST EDITIONS

BIBLIOGRAPHY

1.
The Pothunters
1902. A&C BLACK. 272 pages.
Printed by M'Farlane & Erskine, Edinburgh.

Royal blue cloth, decorated with a silver cup on cover and spine. Ten black-and-white illustrations by R. Noel Pocock. There are two later issues, one with eight pages of advertisements, and one with pictorial boards. Novel.

2.
A Prefect's Uncle
1903. A&C BLACK. 264 pages.
Uncredited Printer.

Red cloth, decorated with lilac and pink. The title appears on the spine within a gold square, above a moustachioed cricketer. Eight black-and-white illustrations by R. Noel Pocock. Novel.

3.
Tales of St. Austin's
1903. A&C BLACK. 282 pages.
Printed by M'Farlane & Erskine, Edinburgh.

There are two different coloured bindings to this first edition – red cloth, decorated with black and lilac, and green cloth, decorated with black and pale blue. The depiction is identical, as is the book internally. The cover and spine bear only the words 'St. Austin's', though the full title appears on the title-page. Twelve black-and-white illustrations by T.M.R. Whitwell, R. Noel Pocock, and E.F. Skinner. Stories.

4.
The Gold Bat
1904. A&C BLACK. 277 pages.
Uncredited Printer.

Wine pictorial cloth, decorated with pale blue, yellow and black. Eight illustrations by T.M.R. Whitwell. Novel.

5.
William Tell Told Again
1904. A&C BLACK. 106 pages.
Printed by Billing & Sons Ltd, Guildford.

Rusty brown cloth, decorated with green, yellow and black. Sixteen full colour illustrations by Philip Dadd. The first edition is considerably slimmer than later, very similar editions, and bears the date. Only reprints have the address of the Publisher.

6.
The Head of Kay's
1905. A&C BLACK. 280 pages.
Printed by M'Farlane & Erskine, Edinburgh.

Red pictorial cloth, decorated with grey, black and yellow. Eight black-and-white illustrations by T.M.R. Whitwell. Novel.

7.
Love among the Chickens
1906. NEWNES. 312 pages.
Printed by Ballantine Hanson & Co., Edinburgh & London.

Beige pictorial cloth, decorated with green, orange, black and yellow. Four line drawings by H.M. Brock. P.G.'s first novel not written for adolescents. A love story.

7. (i)
Love among the Chickens
1909. CIRCLE PUBLISHING CO., New York. 350 pages.

Brown cloth, decorated with black and red. Six illustrations by Armand Both.

7. (ii)
Love among the Chickens
1921. HERBERT JENKINS. 256 pages.

Blue cloth, lettered in a darker blue. The title page bears the words: 'Entirely rewritten for this edition'. Only six previous titles should appear on the verso of the half-title, ending with 'Indiscretions of Archie.'

8.
The White Feather
1907. A&C BLACK. 284 pages.
Uncredited Printer.

Tan cloth, decorated with brown, black and white. Twelve black-and-white illustrations by W. Townend. Novel.

9.
Not George Washington
1907. CASSELL. 279 pages.
Printed by Cassell & Co.

Rust cloth, lettered in gold. Full colour frontispiece by John E. Sutcliffe. This novel was written in collaboration with Herbert Westbrook, and on both the cover and the title page, Wodehouse's name follows that of Westbrook.

10.
The Globe By the Way Book
1908. GLOBE PUBLISHING CO., London. 144 pages.

A collection of the 'By the Way' column, published in *The Globe* newspaper, and written by Wodehouse and Westbrook (See No.9). Scarlet pictorial paper wrappers, decorated with white.

11.
The Swoop
1909. ALSTON RIVERS. 122 pages.
Printed by William Clowes & Sons.

Orange pictorial paper wrappers, decorated with black and white. Thirty textual illustrations by C. Harrison. Novel.

12.
Mike
1909. A&C BLACK. 339 pages.
Printed by Ballantyne & Co. Ltd.

Green pictorial cloth, decorated with white, black and red. Twelve black-and-white illustrations by T.M.R. Whitwell. Novel. A&C Black reissued MIKE in at least two different bindings during the twenties – one plain red, one sky blue, decorated with brown and navy – and with new colour illustrations. They also reissued the second part as ENTER PSMITH, in 1935. The two parts were revised in 1953, and published separately by Herbert Jenkins as MIKE AT WRYKYN and MIKE AND PSMITH.

13.
The Intrusion of Jimmy
1910. W.J. WATT & CO., New York. 314 pages.

Black cloth with a circular, pictorial label, and gold lettering. Five illustrations by Will Grefe. Novel.

13. (i)
A Gentleman of Leisure
1910. ALSTON RIVERS. 352 pages.

Blue cloth, lettered in gold. This, with minor alterations, is simply the English edition of No. 13.

14.
Psmith in the City
1910. A&C BLACK. 266 pages.
Printed by Ballantyne & Co. Ltd.

Blue pictorial cloth, decorated with cream and white. Twelve black-and-white illustrations by T.M.R. Whitwell. Novel.

15.
The Prince and Betty
1912. W.J. WATT & CO., New York. 302 pages.

Black cloth, bearing two coloured ovals, and lettered in gold. Five illustrations by Will Grefe. Novel.

15. (i)
The Prince and Betty
1912. MILLS AND BOON. 282 pages.
Printed by Turnbull & Spears, Edinburgh.

Red cloth, with black lettering on the cover, and gold lettering on the spine. Although the English edition of No.15, the book was utterly rewritten. The later, and undated, Newnes reissue is often mistaken for the first edition.

16.
The Little Nugget
1913. METHUEN. 303 pages.
Printed by Morrison & Gibb, Edinburgh.

Red cloth, blind-stamped on the cover, and decorated in gold on the spine. Novel.

16. (i)
The Little Nugget
1914. W.J. WATT & CO., New York. 300 pages.

Black cloth, decorated with gold. Three illustrations by Will Grefe.

17.
The Man Upstairs
1914. METHUEN. 316 pages.

Brown cloth, with spine decorated in gold. Stories.

18.

Something New
1915. D. APPLETON & CO., New York.
350 pages.

Red cloth, decorated with green and gold. Four illustrations by F.R. Gruger. The first of the Blandings novels.

18. (i)

Something Fresh
1915. METHUEN. 315 pages.
Printed by Butler & Tanner.

Dark green cloth, lettered in black.
This is the (slightly altered) English edition of No. 18, although in the adverts at the rear, Methuen refer to the book as SOMETHING NEW.

19.

Psmith Journalist
1915. A&C BLACK. 247 pages.
Printed by The Complete Press.

French blue pictorial cloth, decorated with black, mustard and cream. Twelve black-and-white illustrations by T.M.R. Whitwell. Novel. A re-write of No. 15.

20.

Uneasy Money
1916. D. APPLETON & CO., New York.
326 pages.

Red cloth decorated with gold. Eight illustrations by Clarence F. Underwood. Novel.

20. (i)

Uneasy Money
1917. METHUEN. 279 pages.
Printed by Butler & Tanner.

Red cloth, lettered in black.

21.

Piccadilly Jim
1917. DODD, MEAD & CO., New York.
364 pages.

Orange cloth, lettered in black. Eight illustrations by May Wilson Preston. Novel.

21. (i)

Piccadilly Jim
1918. HERBERT JENKINS. 316 pages.
Printed by Wm Brendon & Son Ltd.

Mustard cloth, lettered in black. P.G.'s first work with Jenkins.

22.

The Man with Two Left Feet
1917. METHUEN. 297 pages.
Printed by Jarrold & Sons Ltd., Norwich.

Light red cloth, with black lettering. Stories. The story 'Extricating Young Gussie' is the very first Jeeves – Wooster extravaganza.

22. (i)

The Man with Two Left Feet
1933. A.L. BURT & CO., New York.
284 pages.

Orange cloth, with black lettering. Although sixteen years after the English edition, there are three extra stories.

23.

My Man Jeeves
1919. NEWNES. 251 pages.
Printed by Butler & Tanner.

Red cloth, blind-stamped with a hasp design on cover, and decorated and lettered in black on spine.
This is the first book to have the word 'Jeeves' in the title, though only four of the eight stories concern him. The volume is Penguin-sized, though hardcover, and part of the Newnes 1/9d Novels collection.

24.

Their Mutual Child
1919. BONI & LIVERIGHT, New York.
284 pages.

Grey cloth with white lettering. Novel.

24. (i)

The Coming of Bill
1920. HERBERT JENKINS. 251 pages.
Printed by William Clowes & Sons Ltd.

Red cloth, lettered in black. The English edition of No. 24.

Dust-wrapper : Old lady in drophead limousine staring beadily at orange-haired young man whom she has just knocked down.

25.

A Damsel in Distress
1919. GEORGE H. DORAN, New York.
302 pages.

Brown cloth, decorated with orange and black. Novel.

25. (i)

A Damsel in Distress
1919. HERBERT JENKINS. 319 pages.
Printed by Butler & Tanner.

Two bindings exist: wine red and sky blue – both lettered in black.

Dust-wrapper : No sign of a damsel here, but much to the delight of the hoi polloi on the spine, a morning-suited cove is slapped down by an anonymous hand.

26.
The Little Warrior
1920. GEORGE H. DORAN, New York.
383 pages.

Tan cloth, lettered in green. Novel.

26. (i)
Jill the Reckless
1921. HERBERT JENKINS. 313 pages.
Printed by The Mayflower Press.

Blue cloth, lettered in black.
This is the English edition of No. 26. The
green-bound 1922 edition is often mistaken for
the first.

27.
Indiscretions of Archie
1921. HERBERT JENKINS. 320 pages.
Printed by Butler & Tanner.

Pale blue cloth, lettered in black. Stories.

Dust-wrapper : A pater and his pretty offspring
standing waist-deep in Archie's topper, pater
waving a fist at the said Drone, who seems to
care not a jot.

27. (i)
Indiscretions of Archie
1921. GEORGE H. DORAN, New York.
306 pages.

Brown cloth, decorated with green.

28.
The Clicking of Cuthbert
1922. HERBERT JENKINS. 256 pages.
Printed by Love & Malcomson Ltd.

Sage stippled cloth, decorated and lettered in
dark green. Golf stories.

Dust-wrapper : Winsome lass in golfing gear,
her golf bag devoid of niblicks, but brimming
with eligible young men.

28. (i)
Golf without Tears
1924. GEORGE H. DORAN, New York.
330 pages.

Green cloth, lettered in darker green. The
Doran colophon appears beneath the
Copyright details.
With very slight alterations, this is the
American edition of No. 28.

29.
Three Men and a Maid
1922. GEORGE H. DORAN, New York.
304 pages.

Brown cloth, with darker brown lettering on
the spine. The Doran colophon appears
beneath the Copyright details. Novel.

29. (i)
The Girl on the Boat
1922. HERBERT JENKINS. 312 pages.
Printed by Love & Malcomson Ltd.

Orange cloth, decorated and lettered in
maroon. The first lists eight Wodehouse titles
on the verso of the half-title, the last of which
is *The Clicking of Cuthbert.*
A revised edition of No. 29, containing a new
Preface.

Dust-wrapper : There's a knight in armour, you
see, and a girl pointing a rifle at him. On the
spine, a black-and-white minstrel trills along.

30.
The Adventures of Sally
1922. HERBERT JENKINS. 312 pages.
Printed by The Garden City Press, Letchworth.

Orange cloth, decorated and lettered in maroon.
Although published in October 1922, the title
page bears the date MCMXXIII. Novel.

Dust-wrapper : On the spine, Sally is sitting on
a trunk. On the cover, she is stepping on a
be-spatted toe. Its owner is not pleased.

30. (i)
Mostly Sally
1923. GEORGE H. DORAN, New York.
318 pages.

Green cloth, with wine lettering on the spine.
The Doran colophon appears beneath the
Copyright details. The American edition of
No. 30.

31.
The Inimitable Jeeves
1923. HERBERT JENKINS. 255 pages.
Printed by Wyman & Sons Ltd.

Sage cloth, decorated and lettered in dark
green. The first lists ten Wodehouse titles on
the verso of the half-title, ending with *The
Clicking of Cuthbert.* Stories.
One of the best-known stories in this collection,
'The Great Sermon Handicap', was reissued
singly in the early 1930's by Hodder &
Stoughton, in their *Little Books of Laughter*
series. About $4\frac{1}{2} \times 3\frac{1}{2}$ in ($11\frac{1}{2} \times 9$cm), the book
is red cloth, decorated and lettered in gold, and
also printed by Wyman & Sons Ltd.

Dust-wrapper : A uniquely sprightly Jeeves is
chasing a pot-bellied bellboy in such a manner
that one is not at all sure one would care to
imitate.

31. (i)
Jeeves
1923. GEORGE H. DORAN, New York.
288 pages.

Tan cloth, lettered in black. The Doran colophon appears beneath the Copyright details. The American edition of No. 31.

32.
Leave it to Psmith
1923. HERBERT JENKINS. 327 pages. *Printed by Wyman & Sons Ltd.*

Sage cloth, decorated and lettered in black. Eleven Wodehouse titles appear on the verso of the half-title, ending with *Love Among the Chickens*. Novel.
The 1924 edition can be mistaken for the first, though here there are twelve titles listed, including *Ukridge*.

Dust-wrapper : A frightened-looking girl with a nightlight confronts Psmith, squatting in full evening dress and holding a revolver. Good grief.

32. (i)
Leave it to Psmith
1924. GEORGE H. DORAN, New York. 348 pages.
Blue cloth, lettered in black. The Doran colophon appears beneath the Copyright details. The American edition of No. 32.

33.
Ukridge
1924. HERBERT JENKINS. 256 pages. *Printed by Butler & Tanner Ltd.*

Green cloth, decorated and lettered in a darker green. The first lists thirteen Wodehouse titles on the verso of the half-title, ending with *Leave it to Psmith*. Stories.
For the record, it is pronounced 'You-cridge.'

Dust-wrapper : The morning-suited groom seems somewhat irate at receiving an overripe tomato in the eye. His bride looks frankly terrified, and not a little bilious.

33. (i)
He Rather Enjoyed It
1926. GEORGE H. DORAN, New York. 316 pages.

Red cloth, lettered in black. The Doran colophon appears beneath the Copyright details. The American edition of No. 33.

34.
Bill the Conqueror
1924. METHUEN. 296 pages. *Printed by Butler & Tanner Ltd.*
Red cloth, lettered in black. Novel.

Dust-wrapper : Bill leaps into a two-seater, encouraged by a cloched young thing, and pursued by a variety of hot-headed worthies.

34. (i)
Bill the Conqueror
1925. GEORGE H. DORAN, New York. 324 pages.

Yellow cloth, lettered in green. The Doran colophon appears beneath the Copyright details. The American edition of No. 34.

35.
Carry On, Jeeves
1925. HERBERT JENKINS. 256 pages. *Printed by Wyman & Sons Ltd.*

Green cloth, decorated and lettered in black. Thirteen Wodehouse titles appear on the verso of the half-title, the last being *The Coming of Bill*. Stories.
Half of the stories originally appeared in No. 23.

Dust-wrapper : A chinned Jeeves stares disapprovingly at a chinless Bertie's taste in neckwear. Bertie appears immoderately terrified, and who wouldn't be ?

35. (i)
Carry On, Jeeves
1927. GEORGE H. DORAN, New York. 316 pages.

Brown cloth, decorated and lettered in orange. The Doran colophon appears beneath the Copyright details. The American edition of No. 35.

36.
Sam the Sudden
1925. METHUEN. 248 pages. *Printed by Butler & Tanner Ltd.*

Red cloth, lettered in black. Novel.

Dust-wrapper : Sam waves a photo of his beloved at his beloved, loses his hat, and incidentally sticks a finger or two into a portly party's nose. How sudden can you get ?

36. (i)
Sam in the Suburbs
1925. GEORGE H. DORAN, New York.

Green cloth, decorated and lettered in darker green. The Doran colophon appears beneath the Copyright details. The American edition of No. 36.

37.
The Heart of a Goof
1926. HERBERT JENKINS. 314 pages. *Printed by Purnell & Sons.*

Green cloth, decorated and lettered in black. The verso of the half-title lists fourteen Wodehouse titles, the last being *The Coming of Bill*. Golf stories.

Dust-wrapper : The Goof belts divots out of the fairway, while a check-suited lady regards the specimen more in pity than in anger.

37. (i)
Divots
1927. GEORGE H. DORAN, New York. 316 pages.

Orange cloth, decorated and lettered in black. The Doran colophon appears beneath the Copyright details. American edition of No. 37.

38.
Hearts and Diamonds
1926.

Written with Laurie Wylie, this is an adaptation of a play by E. Marischka and B. Granichstead. It was produced in London in 1926, and published in the same year by Prowse.

39.
The Play's the Thing
1927. BRENTANO'S, New York.

This is an adaptation of a play by Ferenc Molnar, first produced in New York in 1926.

40.
The Small Bachelor
1927. METHUEN. 251 pages.
Printed by Butler & Tanner Ltd.

Blue cloth, lettered in black. Novel.

Dust-wrapper : The small bachelor confronts an inordinately large dressing table, and attempts to tie his tie. He is a whit away from hanging himself, and one feels he knows this.

40. (i)
The Small Bachelor
1927. GEORGE H. DORAN, New York. 318 pages.

Yellow cloth, decorated and lettered in brown. The Doran colophon appears beneath the Copyright details. The American edition of No. 40.

41.
Meet Mr. Mulliner
1927. HERBERT JENKINS. 312 pages.
Printed by William Clowes & Sons Ltd.

Green cloth, lettered in black. Stories.

Dust-wrapper : Mr Mulliner's Fair-Isle paunch partially obscures a frantic young silhouette being chased by a boor with a pitchfork.

41. (i)
Meet Mr. Mulliner
1928. DOUBLEDAY, DORAN & Co., New York. 308 pages.

Orange cloth, lettered in wine. The American edition of No. 41.

42.
Good Morning Bill
1928. METHUEN. 160 pages.
Printed by Wyman & Sons Ltd.

Blue cloth, lettered in black. Play.

Dust-wrapper : Bill is on a child's rocking horse. He has the goodness to look faintly embarassed, to say nothing of a silly ass.

43.
Money for Nothing
1928. HERBERT JENKINS. 312 pages.
Printed by Purnell & Sons Ltd.

Orange cloth, lettered in black. Novel.

Dust-wrapper : A masked villain decorates the spine, while a chubby old man skips for his life on the cover.

43. (i)
Money for Nothing
1928. DOUBLEDAY DORAN, GARDEN CITY, New York. 336 pages.

Blue cloth, decorated and lettered in orange. The American edition of No. 43.

44.
Mr Mulliner Speaking
1929. HERBERT JENKINS. 320 pages.
Printed by Purnell & Sons Ltd.

Orange cloth, lettered in black. Stories.

Dust-wrapper : A twenties' lady on the spine glances sidelong at the impossibly cherubic Mulliner visage on the cover.

44. (i)
Mr Mulliner Speaking
1930. DOUBLEDAY DORAN, GARDEN CITY, New York. 334 pages.

Blue cloth, decorated and lettered in darker blue. The American edition of No. 44.

45.
Fish Preferred
1929. DOUBLEDAY DORAN, GARDEN CITY, New York. 328 pages.

Brown cloth, lettered in yellow. Novel.

45. (i)
Summer Lightning
1929. HERBERT JENKINS. 318 pages.
Printed by Purnell & Sons Ltd.

Orange cloth, lettered in black. The English edition of No. 45, with an additional Preface.

Dust-wrapper : A gypsy caravan sits docilely on the spine, while on the cover white lightning sparks from a monocled gent's quill pen.

46.
A Damsel in Distress
1930. FRENCH. 88 pages.
Printed by Butler & Tanner Ltd.

Pale blue paper wrappers, lettered in black.
Play, written in collaboration with Ian Hay.

47.
Baa, Baa, Black Sheep
1930. FRENCH. 88 pages.
Printed by Butler & Tanner Ltd.

Pale blue paper wrappers, lettered in black.
Play, written in collaboration with Ian Hay.

48.
Very Good, Jeeves
1930. DOUBLEDAY, DORAN, GARDEN CITY, New York. 342 pages.

Orange cloth, lettered in black. Stories.

48. (i)
Very Good, Jeeves
1930. HERBERT JENKINS. 312 pages.
Printed by Purnell & Sons Ltd.

Orange cloth, lettered in black.
The English edition of No. 48, with an additional Preface.

Dust-wrapper : On the spine, Bertie is just discovering that the last ring over the swimming pool has been looped back, while on the cover a gigantic Jeeves remains implacable, even if he does rather resemble Frankenstein.

49.
Big Money
1931. DOUBLEDAY, DORAN, GARDEN CITY, New York. 316 pages.

Orange cloth, with green surround to orange lettering. Novel.

49. (i)
Big Money
1931. HERBERT JENKINS. 314 pages.
Printed by Wyman & Sons Ltd.

Orange cloth, lettered in black.

Dust-wrapper : A young couple looks delighted, up to their elbows in banknotes. And why wouldn't they? On the spine hangs a faceless beard.

50.
If I Were You
1931. DOUBLEDAY, DORAN, GARDEN CITY, New York. 306 pages.

Orange cloth, lettered in brown. Novel.

50. (i)
If I Were You
1931. HERBERT JENKINS. 280 pages.
Printed by Wyman & Sons Ltd.

Orange cloth, lettered in black.
The English edition of No. 50.

Dust-wrapper : The incognito and top-hatted Earl shaves a young man on the cover, while on the spine a pair of scissors cross a coronet. The design is by W. Heath Robinson.

51.
Jeeves Omnibus
1931. HERBERT JENKINS. 847 pages.
Printed by Ebenezer Baylis and Son Ltd.

Green cloth, decorated and lettered in black. The frontispiece is a photograph of P.G., looking as if he has been quite recently arrested for doing something reasonably silly.

52.
Leave it to Psmith
1932. FRENCH. 90 pages.
Printed by Butler & Tanner Ltd.

Grey paper wrappers, lettered in black. Play, written in association with Ian Hay.

53.
Louder and Funnier
1932. FABER & FABER. 286 pages.
Printed by Butler & Tanner.

Yellow cloth, lettered in green on the spine.
Humorous articles.
A later issue exists, bound in green cloth in the style of the Faber Library series.

Dust-wrapper : A brilliant design by Rex Whistler depicts P.G. as a be-plinthed neo-Roman bust, laughing as is fit to.

54.
Doctor Sally
1932. METHUEN. 155 pages.
Printed by Jarrold & Sons.

Blue cloth, lettered in black. Novel.

Dust-wrapper : Sally is wearing a black topper. She holds a gooey red heart and listens to it via a stethoscope. Its owner surveys the scene, greenly. Losing one's heart can only lead to pain.

55.
Hot Water
1932. HERBERT JENKINS. 312 pages.
Printed by Wyman & Sons Ltd.

Orange cloth, lettered in black. Novel.

Dust-wrapper : J. Wellington Gedge points at the young couple with both a finger, and a cigar. But they don't care.

55. (i)
Hot Water
1932. DOUBLEDAY, DORAN, GARDEN CITY, New York. 308 pages.

Black cloth, decorated and lettered in orange.
Six illustrations by Rea Irvin.
Neither No. 55 nor No. 55(i) precedes, as they were both published on the 17th August.

56.
Nothing but Wodehouse
1932. DOUBLEDAY, DORAN, GARDEN CITY, New York.

Anthology of reprinted material.

57.
Mulliner Nights
1933. HERBERT JENKINS. 312 pages.
Printed by Wyman & Sons Ltd.

Orange cloth, lettered in black. Stories.

Dust-wrapper : A bald and white-moustachioed pompous-looking Egg pouts on the spine, while Mulliner reclines across the cover, with his pipe.

57. (i)
Mulliner Nights
1933. DOUBLEDAY, DORAN, GARDEN CITY, New York. 312 pages.

Orange cloth, decorated and lettered in black.
The American edition of No. 57.

58.
Heavy Weather
1933. LITTLE, BROWN & CO., Boston. 316 pages.

Black cloth, decorated and lettered in red.
Novel.

58. (i)
Heavy Weather
1933. HERBERT JENKINS. 311 pages.
Printed by Wyman & Sons Ltd.

Pale blue cloth, lettered in orange.
The English edition of No. 58.

Dust-wrapper : On the spine, a butler beats a gong, while on the cover a comely wench finds it hard to suppress a smile over the fact that a black pig is sitting in the rain and grinning like a fool.

59.
Candlelight
1934. FRENCH, New York.

An adaptation of a play by Siegfried Geyer.
Grey paper wrappers, lettered in black.

60.
A Century of Humour
1934. HUTCHINSON. 1024 pages.
Printed by the Hutchinson Printing Trust Ltd.

Yellow cloth, decorated and lettered in black.
Anthology of dozens of authors, edited by P.G.

Dust-wrapper : A jester presides over a list of the biggest names contained in the volume. The wrapper is scarce, due to the fact that it exhorts the reader to remove it, and cut out the book-order forms printed on the reverse – which many, clearly, did.

61.
Methuen's Library of Humour:
P.G. Wodehouse
1934. METHUEN. 153 pages.
Printed by Jarrold & Sons Ltd.

Brown cloth, with blind-stamped design on cover and gold lettering on spine. An anthology of P.G., edited by E.V. Knox.

Dust-wrapper : A decorative border, featuring a king, a policeman, a golfer, a poet, a child, Sir Robert Peel, and a swastika'd Nazi (!).

62.
Thank You, Jeeves
1934. HERBERT JENKINS. 312 pages.
Printed by Wyman & Sons Ltd.

Buff cloth, lettered in red. The first Jeeves novel.

Dust-wrapper : Jeeves raises the eyebrow at the sight of the young master totally flummoxed by the sight of a blonde in bed. Yes, in bed.

62. (i)
Thank You, Jeeves
1934. LITTLE, BROWN & CO., Boston. 308 pages.

Plum cloth, with black lettering.
The American edition of No. 62.

63.
Right Ho, Jeeves
1934. HERBERT JENKINS. 312 pages.
Printed by Wyman & Sons Ltd.

Silver-grey cloth, lettered in red. Novel.

Dust-wrapper : Jeeves retains his cool in the foreground, while Anatole sits up in bed and and goes berserk in mauve-striped pyjamas. Anatole is foreign.

63. (i)
Brinkley Manor
1934. LITTLE, BROWN & CO., Boston. 321 pages.

Red cloth, decorated and lettered in black.
The American edition of No. 63.

64.
Mulliner Omnibus
1935. HERBERT JENKINS. 864 pages.
Printed by Purnell and Sons Ltd.

Green cloth, decorated and lettered in black
(uniform with No. 51) – as is the mug-shot
frontispiece.

65.
Blandings Castle
1935. HERBERT JENKINS. 311 pages.
Printed by Wyman & Sons Ltd.

Chlorophyll cloth, lettered in black. Stories.

Dust-wrapper : A young lady and her beau
caress the grotesque and monumental head of
the Empress – which, disembodied, hovers in
a cloudless sky.

65. (i)
Blandings Castle
1935. DOUBLEDAY, DORAN, GARDEN CITY,
New York. 312 pages.

Green cloth, lettered in darker green.
The American edition of No. 65.

66.
The Luck of the Bodkins
1935. HERBERT JENKINS. 311 pages.
Printed by Wyman & Sons Ltd.

Red cloth, lettered in black. Novel.

Dust-wrapper : The lady appears apprehensive.
The fat old chap champs on his cigar, with
menace. Monty Bodkin, meanwhile, looks as if
he hasn't a care in the world. Which he has,
of course.

66. (i)
The Luck of the Bodkins
1936. LITTLE, BROWN & CO., Boston.
300 pages.

Green cloth, lettered in navy.
A rewritten version of No. 66.

67.
Anything Goes
1936. FRENCH.

A play, written in collaboration with other
hands, and with music by Cole Porter.

68.
Young Men In Spats
1936. HERBERT JENKINS. 312 pages.
Printed by Wyman & Sons Ltd.

Green cloth, lettered in black. Stories.

Dust-wrapper : A tall young man in tails makes
his excuses to a bevy of dressing-gowned
complainers, and a Peke. He is not wearing
spats, but a pair appears on the rear of the

wrapper, thank God. The spine informs us that
this is 'The Drones Club Book of the Month.'

68. (i)
Young Men in Spats
1936. DOUBLEDAY, DORAN, GARDEN CITY,
New York. 298 pages.

Green cloth, lettered in darker green.
There are three new stories in this American
edition, though two others that appear in
No. 68 have been omitted.

69.
Laughing Gas
1936. HERBERT JENKINS. 311 pages.
Printed by Wyman & Sons Ltd.

Dark red cloth, lettered in black. Novel.

Dust-wrapper : Half-a-dozen bimbos engulfed
in a pinky cloud. And yes, they're laughing.

69. (i)
Laughing Gas
1936. DOUBLEDAY, DORAN, GARDEN CITY,
New York. 304 pages.

Orange cloth, lettered in black.
The American edition of No. 69.

70.
The Three Musketeers
1937. CHAPPELL (U.K.) and HARMS (U.S.).
A play written with Clifford Grey and George
Grossmith, with music by Rudolf Friml.

71.
Lord Emsworth and Others
1937. HERBERT JENKINS. 312 pages.
Printed by Wyman & Sons Ltd.

Red cloth, lettered in black. Stories.

Dust-wrapper : The Ninth Earl beams genially
and holds his pince-nez – as well he might, for
a volatile blonde is aiming a rifle at a young
man's bottom.

71. (i)
Crime Wave at Blandings
1937. DOUBLEDAY, DORAN, GARDEN CITY,
New York. 330 pages.

Green cloth, decorated and lettered in darker
green.
The American edition of No. 71.

72.
Summer Moonshine
1937. DOUBLEDAY, DORAN, GARDEN CITY,
New York. 326 pages.

Yellow cloth, decorated and lettered in green.
Novel.

72. (i)
Summer Moonshine
1938. HERBERT JENKINS. 312 pages.
Printed by Wyman & Sons Ltd.

Red cloth, lettered in black.
The English edition of No. 72.

Dust-wrapper : A quarter-moon looks down
upon the scene: an irate knight is brandishing
a whip at a young chap in a striped blazer. His
girlfriend seems delighted, the young man less
so. On the spine, the moon has become full
and gormless.

73.
The Code of the Woosters
1938. HERBERT JENKINS. 312 pages.
Printed by Wyman & Sons Ltd.

Emerald cloth, lettered in black. Novel.

Dust-wrapper : A rakish Wooster and a quite
featureless Jeeves tool along in the
two-seater. A casual cow glows on the spine.

73. (i)
The Code of the Woosters
1938. DOUBLEDAY, DORAN, GARDEN CITY,
New York. 298 pages.

Yellow cloth, decorated and lettered in blue.
Neither No. 73 nor No. 73(i) precedes, as they
were both published on the same date,
October 7th.

74.
Week-end Wodehouse
1939. HERBERT JENKINS (U.K.) and
DOUBLEDAY, DORAN, GARDEN CITY, New
York (U.S.). 508 pages.
Printed by Purnell & Sons Ltd.

Green cloth, with facsimile signature in gold
on cover, and gold lettering within green
leather label on spine. Anthology, introduced
by Hilaire Belloc, and illustrated by Kerr.

75.
Uncle Fred in the Springtime
1939. DOUBLEDAY, DORAN, GARDEN CITY,
New York. 296 pages.

Green cloth, decorated and lettered in brown.
Novel.

75. (i)
Uncle Fred in the Springtime
1939. HERBERT JENKINS. 311 pages.
Printed by Wyman & Sons Ltd.

Red cloth, lettered in gold on the spine.
The English edition of No. 75.

Dust-wrapper : Purple-faced, white-
moustachioed and cigar-smoking Uncle Fred
views the porcine pride of Blandings, who has

the monogram and coronet tastefully
embroidered upon her rump.

76.
Wodehouse on Golf
1940. DOUBLEDAY, DORAN, GARDEN CITY,
New York.

Anthology of stories.

77.
Eggs, Beans and Crumpets
1940. HERBERT JENKINS. 284 pages.
Printed by Wyman & Sons Ltd.

Orange cloth, lettered in black. Stories.

Dust-wrapper : A green window-pane check-
suited Egg, and a tan herringbone-suited Bean
are strolling Drones-wards. They are, naturally
enough, about to be assaulted by a toppered
portly type, emerging from a casual taxi.

77. (i)
Eggs, Beans and Crumpets
1940. DOUBLEDAY, DORAN, GARDEN CITY,
New York. 312 pages.

Green cloth, decorated and lettered in darker
green.
The American edition of No. 77, though with
a different selection of stories.

78.
Quick Service
1940. HERBERT JENKINS. 252 pages.
Printed by Wyman & Sons Ltd.

There are two bindings: Red cloth, lettered in
gold, and orange cloth, lettered in black. Novel.

Dust-wrapper : The tall, slim and younger man
points the accusing digit at the short, fat and
older type, who glowers in a stiff shirt-front
and smokes a cigar at the aforesaid and
emaciated blot.

78. (i)
Quick Service
1940. DOUBLEDAY, DORAN, GARDEN CITY,
New York. 312 pages.

Stone cloth, decorated and lettered in black.
The American edition of No. 78.

79.
Money in the Bank
1942. DOUBLEDAY, DORAN, GARDEN CITY,
New York. 304 pages.

Plum cloth, lettered in black. Novel.

79. (i)
Money in the Bank
1946. HERBERT JENKINS. 253 pages.
Printed by Wyman & Sons Ltd.

Orange cloth, lettered in black.
The English edition of No. 79.

Dust-wrapper : In a lush and lilac bedroom, a bald and corpulent butler sees fit to kneel in front of a dressing-table. The shapely Miss at the door seems as amazed as we are.

80.
Joy in the Morning
1946. DOUBLEDAY & CO., GARDEN CITY, New York. 282 pages.

Grey cloth, decorated and lettered in green. Illustrated by Paul Galdone. Jeeves novel.

80. (i)
Joy in the Morning
1947. HERBERT JENKINS. 256 pages.
Printed by Wyman & Sons Ltd.

Orange cloth, lettered in black. No date appears on the verso of the title-page. The English edition of No. 80.

Dust-wrapper : The twittering bird on the branch has most undoubtedly struck a chord with Jeeves, for he raises his bowler and smirks boyishly. Yes. Smirks boyishly.

81.
Full Moon
1947. DOUBLEDAY & CO., GARDEN CITY, New York. 280 pages.

Turquoise cloth, lettered in black, with illustrations by Paul Galdone. Novel.

81. (i)
Full Moon
1947. HERBERT JENKINS. 252 pages.
Printed by Wyman & Sons Ltd.

Orange cloth, lettered in black. No date appears on the verso of the title-page. The English edition of No. 81.

Dust-wrapper : The moon is full, and the bare-shouldered and beautiful lady raises huge eyes to the bespectacled Englishman, who duly simpers with enthusiasm.

82.
Spring Fever
1948. HERBERT JENKINS. 256 pages.
Printed by Wyman & Sons Ltd.

Orange cloth, lettered in black. No date appears on the verso of the title-page. Novel.

Dust-wrapper : It seems as if one or two seasons have passed while the characters from 81's dust-wrapper have not actually got around to budging an inch. The Englishman, though, looks quite close to opening his mouth. One cannot rush these things.

82. (i)
Spring Fever
1948. DOUBLEDAY & CO., GARDEN CITY, New York. 224 pages.

Brown cloth, decorated and lettered in white. Illustrated by Paul Galdone.
Neither the English nor the American edition actually precedes, as both were published on the same date, May 20th.

83.
Uncle Dynamite
1948. HERBERT JENKINS. 249 pages.
Printed by Wyman & Sons Ltd.

Orange cloth, lettered in black. Novel.

Dust-wrapper : On the wall is the mounted head of a tiger, and also that of a gnu, beneath which reposes a disgruntled bust. None of this can stop Uncle Fred beaming, however, as he grasps a stiffish and amber tissue-restorer.

83. (i)
Uncle Dynamite
1948. DIDIER, New York. 312 pages.

Red cloth, lettered in silver. Illustrations by Hal McIntosh.
The American edition of No. 83.

84.
The Best of Wodehouse
1949. POCKET BOOKS, New York.

Anthology.

85.
The Mating Season
1949. HERBERT JENKINS. 246 pages.
Printed by Wyman & Sons Ltd.

Orange cloth, lettered in black. As usual during this period, no date appears on the verso of the title-page. Novel.

Dust-wrapper : Bertie in a scrape. A very no-nonsense lady is pointing a gun! The fact that it looks like a piece of chocolate cake is neither here, and nor is it there.

85. (i)
The Mating Season
1949. DIDIER, New York. 290 pages.

Wine cloth, lettered in silver, and illustrated by Hal McIntosh.
The American edition of No. 85.

86.
Nothing Serious
1950. HERBERT JENKINS. 254 pages.
Printed by Wyman & Sons Ltd.

Orange cloth, lettered in black. No date appears on the verso of the title-page. Stories.

Dust-wrapper : The cover and spine has three smiling chaps, various possessors of a wine-glass, an RAF moustache, and a monocle. None is aware of anything remotely serious.

86. (i)
Nothing Serious
1951. DOUBLEDAY & CO., GARDEN CITY, New York. 224 pages.

Red cloth, lettered in black.
The American edition of No. 86.

87.
The Old Reliable
1951. HERBERT JENKINS. 233 pages.
Printed by Wyman & Sons Ltd.
Orange cloth, lettered in black. A later issue exists, with red boards. No date appears on the verso of the title-page. Novel.

Dust-wrapper : A caddish cove named Smedley ecstatically clutches a yellow, salacious and saleable diary. But lo, Phipps the butler also wants said diary, and is it not he who leers from behind the red drapes? Yes, it is.

87. (i)
The Old Reliable
1951. DOUBLEDAY & CO., GARDEN CITY, New York. 222 pages.

Tan cloth, lettered in red.
The American edition of No. 87.

88.
Best of Modern Humor
1952. McBRIDE, New York. An anthology of humorous writing, edited and introduced by P.G.

89.
The Week-end Book of Humor
1952. WASHBURN, New York. Another anthology of humour, selected by P.G. and Scott Meredith, and introduced by P.G.

89. (i)
The Week-end Book of Humour
1954. HERBERT JENKINS. The English edition of No. 89.

90.
Barmy in Wonderland
1952. HERBERT JENKINS. 222 pages.
Printed by Wyman & Sons Ltd.

Red boards, lettered in black. Novel.

Dust-wrapper : Barmy accompanies a girl with many cherries on her hat. They are in New York, and Barmy is sucking the top of his umbrella. Barmy is only a nickname, of course; his real name is Cyril Fotheringay-Phipps.

90. (i)
Angel Cake
1952. DOUBLEDAY & CO., GARDEN CITY, New York. 224 pages.

Tan cloth, lettered in green.
This is the American edition of No. 90, identical apart from the dedication.

91.
Pigs Have Wings
1952. DOUBLEDAY & CO., GARDEN CITY, New York. 222 pages.

Grey cloth, lettered in white. Novel.

91. (i)
Pigs Have Wings
1952. HERBERT JENKINS. 220 pages.
Printed by Wyman & Sons Ltd.

Red boards, lettered in black.
The English edition of No. 91.

Dust-wrapper : Beach the butler opens the door to a totally self-satisfied Empress of Blandings — or could it be the Pride of Matchingham? Either way, Beach is the one in wing collar and tails.

92.
Mike at Wrykyn
1953. HERBERT JENKINS. 189 pages.
Printed by Wyman & Sons Ltd.

Red boards, lettered in black. One half of a rewrite and reissue of No. 12. Verso of title-page reads: 'First published. . . 1953.'

Dust-wrapper : Mike, looking not at all of the 1950s, strikes out at the wicket, while a mauve-capped wicket-keeper looks sullen and afraid, as wicket-keepers generally do. There is also depicted a fairly silly mid-off.

93.
Mike and Psmith
1953. HERBERT JENKINS. 190 pages.
Printed by Wyman & Sons Ltd.

Red boards, lettered in black. The same applies here as to No. 92, though in this case the verso of the title-page reads: 'Reissued. . . 1953.'

Dust-wrapper : They chat in the quad. Mike, in white flannels, appears relaxed and fifteen. Psmith looks like Fred Astaire with eyebrows, and about forty-five. It could be something to do with the pin-stripes, monocle, and recently polished hair.

94.
Ring for Jeeves
1953. HERBERT JENKINS. 222 pages.
Printed by Wyman & Sons Ltd.

Red boards, lettered in black. Novel.

Dust-wrapper : A pitifully emaciated Jeeves fingers the telephone receiver, and contemplates the wisdom of addressing himself into it. He could be pining for Bertie who doesn't feature in this novel. Though it seems unlikely.

94. (i)
The Return of Jeeves
1954. SIMON & SCHUSTER, New York. 220 pages.

Grey and tan boards, lettered in brown. This is the somewhat altered American edition of No. 94.

95.
Bring on the Girls
1953. SIMON & SCHUSTER, New York. 280 pages.

Black and green boards, decorated and lettered in red and dark green.
This was written with Guy Bolton, and is the (mainly) autobiographical tale of their collaboration in musicals.

95. (i)
Bring on the Girls
1954. HERBERT JENKINS. 248 pages. *Printed by Wyman & Sons Ltd.*

Plum boards, with spine lettered in gold. This is a rewritten version of No. 95, and the photographs differ.

Dust-wrapper : Eighteen eminently resistible chorus-girls flex their knees across the cover, and curve around the spine.

96.
Performing Flea
1953. HERBERT JENKINS. 224 pages. *Printed by Wyman & Sons Ltd.*

Sky blue boards, lettered in gold; the front cover bears a facsimile signature, also in gold. This is a book of letters by P.G., sent to W. Townend over the years of their friendship. It is the nearest P.G. ever got to autobiography.

Dust-wrapper : From a brown background, the black-and-white effigy of Plum stares at us. He doesn't know what to think. He has the air of a man who looks like the before picture in a hair-restorer advert, and knows it.

96. (i)
Author! Author!
1962. SIMON & SCHUSTER, New York. 192 pages.

Yellow boards, lettered in red.
This is the American edition of No. 96, though it was very much revised, and new material was added.

97.
Jeeves and the Feudal Spirit
1954. HERBERT JENKINS. 222 pages. *Printed by Wyman & Sons Ltd.*

Red boards, lettered in black. Novel.

Dust-wrapper : Bertie gazes uncertainly at his strange, unnatural beauty in a monogrammed hand-mirror. The lip sprouts fungus, hence the uncertainty. Jeeves, on the other hand, seems quite decided on the matter.

97. (i)
Bertie Wooster Sees It Through
1955. SIMON & SCHUSTER, New York. 248 pages.

Tan and green boards, lettered in gold and brown.
The American edition of No. 97, identical apart from the addition of a dedication.

98.
Carry on Jeeves
1956. EVANS.

Play. Grey wrappers.

99.
French Leave
1956. HERBERT JENKINS. 206 pages. *Printed by Wyman & Sons Ltd.*

Red cloth, lettered in black. Novel.

Dust-wrapper : The French Marquis chats to a couple of silly American ladies at a cafe table. Their sunglasses are like Cadillacs, poised for a quick getaway.

99. (i)
French Leave
1959. SIMON & SCHUSTER, New York. 216 pages.

Blue boards, decorated and lettered in green and dark blue.
The American edition of No. 99.

100.
America, I Like You
1956. SIMON & SCHUSTER, New York. 212 pages.

Blue boards, cream spine, lettered in red with facsimile signature in blue, Illustrated by Marc Simont.
This book deals with P.G.'s feelings about America, based mainly on a series of Punch articles.

100. (i)
Over Seventy
1957. HERBERT JENKINS. 190 pages.

Red cloth, the spine lettered in gold, the cover bearing a facsimile signature, also in gold.

The rewritten English edition of No. 100, with less about America, and more 'autobiography with digressions.'

Dust-wrapper : A colour photograph of P.G. in his garden, looking under sixty. A suntanned and genial Easter egg, holding a pipe and an impossibly sullen cat.

101.
Something Fishy
1957. HERBERT JENKINS. 198 pages.
Printed by Wyman & Sons Ltd.

Red boards, lettered in black. Novel.

Dust-wrapper : A spiv slouches by a rifled desk, a butler lies prostrate on the ground and is hovered over by a Scrooge-like figure with a monocle, a wing-collar, and a shovel. Something fishy.

101. (i)
The Butler Did It
1957. SIMON & SCHUSTER, New York. 218 pages.

Black and green boards, lettered in silver. The American edition of No. 101.

102.
Selected Stories by P.G. Wodehouse
1958. THE MODERN LIBRARY (RANDOM HOUSE), New York. 382 pages.

Red cloth, with gold lettering and decoration within black rectangles on cover and spine. Introduction by John W. Aldridge.

Dust-wrapper : A line drawing of a pink and silly-looking Jeeves. Bald. And with white mutton-chop side-whiskers. I kid you not.

103.
Cocktail Time
1958. HERBERT JENKINS. 222 pages.
Printed by John Gardner Ltd.

Red boards, lettered in black. Novel.

Dust-wrapper : Uncle Fred, resplendent in dinner jacket and white moustache, has discovered a twelve-inch lady on the end of his cocktail stick. She is wearing a cocktail dress. She is standing on his cherry.

103. (i)
Cocktail Time
1958. SIMON & SCHUSTER, New York. 220 pages.

Black and pink boards, lettered in black and green. The American edition of No. 103.

104.
A Few Quick Ones
1959. SIMON & SCHUSTER, New York. 216 pages.

Grey and white boards, lettered in black and pink. Stories.

104. (i)
A Few Quick Ones
1959. HERBERT JENKINS. 207 pages.
Printed by John Gardner Ltd.

Two bindings exist : red boards lettered in black, and the less common blue boards, also lettered in black. English edition of No. 104, with a different selection of stories.

Dust-wrapper : A montage of everyday life : golf, yellow waistcoats, butlers, cocktails, monocles – oh yes, and red silk dressing-gowns with white spots and quilted lapels.

105.
The Most of P.G. Wodehouse
1960. SIMON & SCHUSTER, New York.

An anthology, edited by P.G.

106.
How Right You Are, Jeeves
1960. SIMON & SCHUSTER, New York. 184 pages.

Orange and white boards, lettered in black. Novel.

106. (i)
Jeeves in the Offing
1960. HERBERT JENKINS. 205 pages.
Printed by Charles Birchall & Sons Ltd.

Red boards, with spine lettered in gold. The half-title reads *A Few Quick Ones*. This error was corrected, subsequent issues of the first edition containing the altered half-title, and bound in beige boards, lettered in black. The English edition of No. 106.

Dust-wrapper : Bertie, the Rev. Aubrey Upjohn and Bobbie Wickham are taking *al fresco* tea at Brinkley Court. The bald and fat butler in attendance, therefore, is not Jeeves at all. Bertie is engaged in the act of spilling his tea over the Rev.'s knees.

107.
The Ice in the Bedroom
1961. SIMON & SCHUSTER, New York. 250 pages.

Black boards, lettered in red, white and yellow. Novel.

107. (i)
Ice in the Bedroom
1961. HERBERT JENKINS. 223 pages.
Printed by William Clowes & Sons Ltd.

Red boards, lettered in gold. Some copies appear with black lettering. The English edition of No. 107.

Dust-wrapper : Probably the worst design ever to appear on a P.G. book. It is shocking pink, and in most other ways as well. There is a blue and silly man in a bowler, and the artist does not reveal his name.

108.
Service with a Smile
1961. SIMON & SCHUSTER, New York. 220 pages.

Black and lilac boards, lettered in white. Novel.

108. (i)
Service with a Smile
1962. HERBERT JENKINS. 192 pages.
Printed by William Clowes & Sons Ltd.

Red cloth, lettered in gold.
The English edition of No. 108.

Dust-wrapper : The Fifth Earl of Ickenham (Uncle Fred) sports a shooting hat, a cigar and a cane. He is riding on the back of the Empress, who is in her turn sucking a daisy. She has a coronet on her bottom.

109.
Stiff Upper Lip, Jeeves
1963. SIMON & SCHUSTER, New York. 224 pages.

Grey boards, lettered in blue and yellow. Novel.

109. (i)
Stiff Upper Lip, Jeeves
1963. HERBERT JENKINS. 189 pages.
Printed by John Gardner Ltd.

Red boards, lettered in gold.
The English edition of No. 109.

Dust-wrapper : Bertie and Jeeves are nose to nose. The Gentleman's gentleman displays the stiff upper lip, and Wooster the loose flabby chin.

110.
Biffen's Millions
1964. SIMON & SCHUSTER, New York. 224 pages.

Red and yellow boards, decorated and lettered in black. Novel.

110. (i)
Frozen Assets
1964. HERBERT JENKINS. 219 pages.
Printed by John Gardner Ltd.

Red boards, lettered in gold.
The English edition of No. 110.

Dust-wrapper : A London copper is bombarded with them. Also half-crowns, halfpennies and florins. This was before the days of p's.

111.
The Brinkmanship of Galahad Threepwood
1965. SIMON & SCHUSTER, New York. 224 pages.

Dark and light yellow boards, decorated and lettered in blue and gold. Novel.

111. (i)
Galahad at Blandings
1965. HERBERT JENKINS. 224 pages.
Printed by Bristol Typesetting Co. Ltd.

Red boards, lettered in gold.
The English edition of No. 111.

Dust-wrapper : It is 1965, and therefore Gally thinks nought of beaming from behind the Blandings turrets, sporting monocle, cigarette holder, wing collar, and spotted tie. And quite right too.

112.
Plum Pie
1966. HERBERT JENKINS. 285 pages.
Printed by Northumberland Press Ltd.

Plum boards, lettered in silver. Stories.

Dust-wrapper : The only typographical wrapper in the P.G. canon. It is plum-coloured, of course, and bears Wodehouse's name in white Playbill, and the title in orange nouveau art nouveau, the whole rather reminiscent of sixties psychedelic carrier bags.

112. (i)
Plum Pie
1967. SIMON & SCHUSTER, New York. 254 pages.

Plum and blue boards, decorated and lettered in silver.
The slightly reduced American edition of No. 112.

113.
A Carnival of Modern Humor
1967. DELACORTE, New York. An anthology of humorous writing, edited by P.G. and Scott Meredith, and introduced by P.G.

113. (i)
A Carnival of Modern Humour
1968. HERBERT JENKINS. The English edition of No. 113.

114.
The World of Jeeves
1967. HERBERT JENKINS. 564 pages.
Printed by Gloucester Typesetting Co. Ltd.

Pale blue boards, lettered in white.
An anthology of all the Jeeves stories. A 'Ninetieth Birthday' edition was reissued in

1971, the dust-wrapper bearing a medallion to this effect.

Dust-wrapper : White, with the word 'Jeeves' in shocking pink, orange and olive letters. Fun is the message, and it works.

115.
The Purloined Paperweight
1967. SIMON & SCHUSTER, New York. 190 pages.
Grey and yellow boards, decorated and lettered in blue. Novel.

115. (i)
Company for Henry
1967. HERBERT JENKINS. 222 pages.
Printed by Northumberland Press Ltd.

Tan boards, lettered in white.
The English edition of No. 115.

Dust-wrapper : Henry, and lady-friend, peruse a letter in the grounds of Ashby Hall. It is hard to say whether the lady's eyes are popping at the letter's contents, or simply because the wrapper is by Osbert Lancaster. The back cover has a photograph of P.G. smoking and reading, just like authors do. This photo also appears on the back of No. 114.

116.
Do Butlers Burgle Banks?
1968. SIMON & SCHUSTER, New York. 192 pages.
Blue and yellow boards, lettered in gold. Novel.

116. (i)
Do Butlers Burgle Banks?
1968. HERBERT JENKINS. 189 pages.
Printed by Northumberland Press Ltd.

Green boards, lettered in silver.
The English edition of No. 116.

Dust-wrapper : Basher the gangster assumes an attitude of prayer. The sight is enough to make the cigar-smoking and green-baize-aproned butler spill his port. And who can blame him ? The design is by Osbert Lancaster, and the rear cover has a photograph of P.G. with his arm in a dovecote, trying to catch the bird. He looks very Americanized now, every garment bearing checks, and then some.

117.
A Pelican at Blandings
1969. HERBERT JENKINS. 222 pages.
Printed by Northumberland Press Ltd.

Black boards, lettered in silver. Novel.

Dust-wrapper : The Duke of Dunstable, in magnificent yellow- and purple-crested pyjamas, seems about ready to slosh the Earl over the head with a bottle of Vichy. On the wall, Landseer's stag is at bay, and the Earl doesn't seem too delighted either. The design is by Osbert Lancaster, and the rear cover bears the remarkable and deathless photograph of P.G. touching his toes.

117. (i)
No Nudes Is Good Nudes
1970. SIMON & SCHUSTER, New York. 220 pages.

Tan and orange boards, lettered in black. Apart from the slight title change, this is the American edition of No. 117.

118.
The Girl in Blue
1970. BARRIE & JENKINS. 192 pages.
Printed by Northumberland Press Ltd.

Blue boards, lettered in gold. Novel.

Dust-wrapper : A pop-eyed Lancaster-Gainsborough oval is surrounded by four pop-eyed Lancaster miniatures. A gallery of rogues, as it happens.

118. (i)
The Girl in Blue
1971. SIMON & SCHUSTER, New York. 190 pages.

Blue boards, lettered in silver.
The American edition of No. 118.

119.
Much Obliged, Jeeves
1971. BARRIE & JENKINS. 192 pages.
Printed by Northumberland Press Ltd.

Blue boards, lettered in gold. Novel.

Dust-wrapper : A balding and portly Jeeves (with side-burns!) discreetly and proudly lights the candles on P.G.'s ninetieth birthday cake. It is seldom a man can so honour his creator.

119. (i)
Jeeves and the Tie That Binds
1971. SIMON & SCHUSTER. 189 pages.

Yellow boards, lettered in black.
The American edition of No. 119. Neither actually precedes, as they were both published precisely on P.G.'s ninetieth birthday – 15th October.

120.
The World of Mr Mulliner
1972. BARRIE & JENKINS. 622 pages.
Printed by Ascot Press Ltd.

Apple green boards, lettered in white.
A reissued, revised and enlarged edition of No. 64, with a new Preface.

Dust-wrapper : The title, in multi-coloured and jocular lettering, against a white ground.

121.
Pearls, Girls and Monty Bodkin
1972. BARRIE & JENKINS. 192 pages.
Printed by Northumberland Press Ltd.

Green boards, lettered in gold. Novel.

Dust-wrapper : A none-too masculine Monty is confronted by a not-overly feminine lady at dusk, outside his door. He is carrying a pipe. She is carrying a gun. He is surprised. Agape, even.

121. (i)
The Plot That Thickened
1973. SIMON & SCHUSTER. 221 pages.

Brown boards, lettered in gold.
The American edition of No. 121.

122.
The Golf Omnibus
1973. BARRIE & JENKINS. 467 pages.
Printed by Redwood Press Ltd.

Chlorophyll boards, lettered in white. A collection of the thirty-one golf stories, with a new Preface.

Dust-wrapper : As No. 120.
In 1974, Simon & Schuster imported a number of the English edition, and distributed it in America.

123.
Bachelors Anonymous
1973. BARRIE & JENKINS. 191 pages.
Printed by Northumberland Press Ltd.

Green boards, lettered in gold. Novel.

Dust-wrapper : An ageing bachelor has his hand bandaged by an ample and comforting woman. He has a thinning crew-cut, rimless spectacles, a button-down shirt, an Art Deco tie with tie-bar, and a brace of cigars protruding from his breast pocket. He is American.

123. (i)
Bachelors Anonymous
1974. SIMON & SCHUSTER. 186 pages.

Blue boards, lettered in silver.
The American edition of No. 123.

124.
The World of Psmith
1974. BARRIE & JENKINS. 597 pages.
Printed by Northumberland Press Ltd.

Green boards, lettered in white. All the Psmith stuff, and a new Preface to boot.

Dust-wrapper : As No. 120, but with an enchanting silhouette of Psmith on the pspine, looking quite the pswell.

125.
Aunts Aren't Gentlemen
1974. BARRIE & JENKINS. 176 pages.
Printed by Clarke, Doble and Brendon Ltd.

Blue boards, lettered in gold. Novel.

Dust-wrapper : Bertie Wooster is about to stroke a cat, and wants to appear natural. He looks bug-eyed and hopeless. A red-faced major is clutching a crop and shouting. He looks very much like Osbert Lancaster, who designed the whole thing.

125. (i)
The Cat-nappers
1975. SIMON & SCHUSTER. 190 pages.

Brown boards, lettered in gold.
The American edition of No. 125.

126.
The World of Ukridge
1975. BARRIE & JENKINS. 286 pages.
Printed by Redwood Burn Ltd.

Red boards, lettered in silver.
All the Ukridge stories.

Dust-wrapper : As No. 120.

127.
The World of Blandings
1976. BARRIE & JENKINS. 357 pages.
Printed by Redwood Burn Ltd.

Black boards, lettered in gold.
Two novels, and three stories.

Dust-wrapper : As No. 120.

128.
The Uncollected Wodehouse
1976. SEABURY PRESS INC, New York.
212 pages.

Blue boards, lettered in silver.
A collection of previously uncollected stories and articles, edited and introduced by David Jasen, and with a Foreword by Malcolm Muggeridge.

Dust-wrapper : A blue and beige sort of Deco-type collage drawing, featuring, one assumes, the face of P.G., looking more like Billy Cotton.

129.
Vintage Wodehouse
1977. BARRIE & JENKINS. 287 pages.
Printed by The Anchor Press Ltd.

Blue boards, lettered in gold.
An anthology of Plum's, edited by Richard Usborne.

Dust-wrapper : Deco artwork, featuring Emsworth, The Empress, Bertie, and some unidentified blot on the landscape – probably someone or other's fiancée.

130.
Sunset at Blandings
1977. CHATTO & WINDUS. 213 pages.
Printed by Ebenezer Baylis & Son Ltd.

Turquoise boards, lettered in gold.
The last, unfinished novel, edited by Richard Usborne.

Dust-wrapper : The entire cast is assembled on the Blandings lawns as the sun dips down behind the Castle turrets, for the last time.

In addition, Wodehouse had stories published in the following anthologies (first appearance in book form):

The Funny Bone SCRIBNERS, NY 1928
The Legion Book CASSELL 1929
The Cecil Aldin Book EYRE & SPOTTISWOODE 1932
The First Time I CHAPMAN & HALL 1935
The Laughter Omnibus FABER & FABER 1937

Wodehouse contributed Prefaces or Forewords to the following:

Charles Graves **And the Greeks** BLES 1930
Herbert Jenkins **Bindle Omnibus** JENKINS 1932
Will Cuppy **How to Tell Your Friends from the Apes** METHUEN 1934
Guy Bolton **Gracious Living Limited** Jenkins 1966

MAGAZINES AND PERIODICALS

Between the years 1901 and 1970, Wodehouse contributed hundreds of stories and articles to magazines. A checklist of the titles of these appears at the rear of Jasen's biography. Here follows a list of all the magazines in which Wodehouse's work appeared.

Public School Magazine
The Captain
Ainslee's
The Strand
Cosmopolitan
Colliers
London Magazine
Ladies Home Journal
Pearsons
McClure's
The Century
The Red Book
The Saturday Evening Post
Chicago Tribune

Elk's Magazine
Liberty
The American
This Week
Harper's Bazaar
Playboy
National Home Monthly
The Bluebook
Punch
Escapade
Ellery Queen
Argosy
The Saint Mystery Magazine

BOOKS ABOUT P.G. WODEHOUSE

Wodehouse at Work
Richard Usborne. HERBERT JENKINS. 1961.

P.G. Wodehouse
R.B.D. French. OLIVER & BOYD. 1966.

P.G. Wodehouse
Richard J. Voorhees. TWAYNE, U.S. 1966.

Wooster's World
Geoffrey Jaggard. MACDONALD. 1967.

Blandings the Blest
Geoffrey Jaggard. MACDONALD. 1968.

**A Bibliography and Reader's Guide
to the First Editions of P.G. Wodehouse**
David A. Jasen. BARRIE & JENKINS. 1971.

The World of P.G. Wodehouse
Herbert Warren Wind. PRAEGER, U.S. 1972.

Homage to P.G. Wodehouse
Ed. Thelma Cazalet-Keir. BARRIE & JENKINS. 1973.

The Comic Style of P.G. Wodehouse
Robert A. Hall Jr. ARCHON, U.S. 1974.

P.G. Wodehouse: a Portrait of a Master
David A. Jasen. GARNSTONE PRESS. 1975.

P.G. Wodehouse
Owen Dudley Edwards. BRIAN O'KEEFE. 1977.

Wodehouse at Work to the End
Richard Usborne. BARRIE & JENKINS. 1977.
(Revised and supplemented 1961 edition)

Dr Sir Pelham Wodehouse Old Boy
Richard Usborne. *Privately Printed*. 1978.
(Limited to 500 copies, 100 of which numbered and signed)

The Wodehouse Companion
Richard Usborne. HAMISH HAMILTON. 1979

Jeeves
C. Northcote-Parkinson. MACDONALD & JANE'S. 1979

PHOTOGRAPHIC ACKNOWLEDGMENTS

Barrie & Jenkins 2, 25, 28, 30, 42, 44, 55, 69, 90, 106, 114, 116, 124/5.   BBC Copyright 118, 119, 120, 121, 122, 123, 126.   Bettmann Archive, The 60, 72, 110.   Camera Press 116.   Cazalet-Keir, Mrs. T. 94.   Compix 63, 74, 76, 85, 98, 101 (above).   Daily Mirror/Syndication International 92.   Dulwich College 16, 20, 134.   Faber & Faber/The Rex Whistler Estate 10.   Angelo Hornak 22, 28, 30, 42, 55, 69, 106, 114.   Keystone 82.   Kobal Collection, The 58, 61 (below),/MGM 78,/RKO Radio Pictures 80, 81.   Lancaster, Sir Osbert 114.   Courtesy Madame Tussaud's London 130 (below right).   Mander and Mitchenson Theatre Collection 40, 45, 54.   Popperfoto 67 (above), 112.   Radio Times Hulton Picture Library 19, 32, 38, 39, 46, 50/1, 53, 57, 61 (above left), 64/5, 67 (below), 70, 97.   Copyright Vernon Richards/Orwell Archive University College London 101 (below).   Reprinted from The Saturday Evening Post © 1915, 1925 The Curtis Publishing Co. 36, 48.   Wide World Photos 61 (above right), 109, 117, 129, 130 (above, below left), 132.

INDEX